LUFTWERK
INSITE
05/02–07/29/2016

ASSAF EVRON
MIES WINDOWS – CROWN HALL, CHICAGO
09/09/2016–01/20/2017

REBECCA WILTON
LA FAYETTE, DETROIT
01/25–06/02/2017

CHRISTINA WILDGRUBE
RESIDENZ / SIEDLUNG TÖRTEN
07/24–08/18/2017

ANKE LOH
INTERKNIT
08/28–10/20/2017

DOUG FOGELSON
FORMS & RECORDS
10/27–12/31/2017

AF623053

ASSAF EVRON
COLLAGES
01/18–04/06/2018

SERENE WISE
STUDIES IN GRAYS AND WHITE
04/11–06/29/2018

HEIKE ALBRECHT
RESIDENZ / SPURENBEWEGUNG
07/16–09/14/2018

MONIKA WULFERS
LINES AND NUMBERS
09/17–12/31/2018

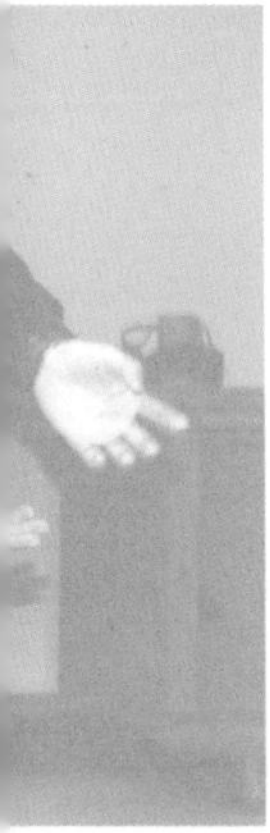

A LITTLE PIECE OF BAUHAUS

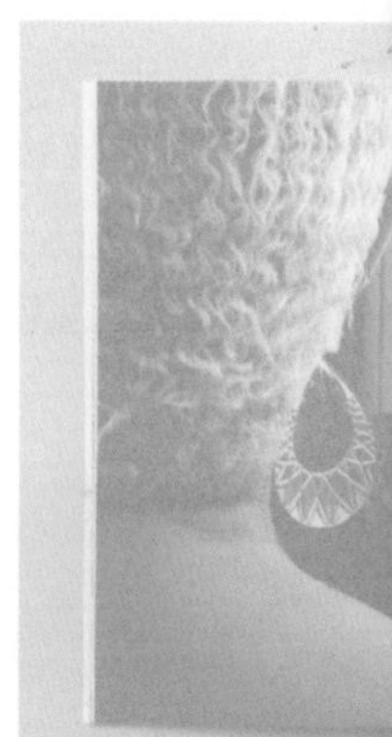

KERBER

GOETHE
INSTITUT

EIN STÜCK BAUHAUS

KERBER ART

GOETHE INSTITUT

CONTENT

INHALT

A LITTLE PIECE OF BAUHAUS

Petra Roggel
Director of the Goethe-Institut Chicago

Irmi Maunu-Kocian
Program coordinator at the Goethe-Institut Chicago

Our exhibition series, which we called A Little Piece of Bauhaus, *took place at the Goethe-Institut Chicago between May 2016 and December 2018. The idea was to combine the two Bauhaus anniversaries with a series of exhibitions during this time: Eighty years of the Chicago Bauhaus in 2017 and 100 years of the Bauhaus in Germany in 2019. Our small exhibition space cannot compete with the big institutions in the city. We could offer the artists one small wall in our entrance area, just opposite the reception desk. Ergo the title* A Little Piece of Bauhaus, *because there was no space here for larger works.*

Another idea was to use these exhibitions to get in touch with artists from Chicago and Germany and allow them to get in touch with us. We wanted to act as an open medium, not planning far into the future. For example, one regular visitor turned out to be an artist who had owned a studio for years in one of the oldest artists' buildings on Michigan Avenue, the Fine Arts Building – a high-rise that still has elevator operators – and one day she simply invited us to visit her. Her work immediately reminded us of Bauhaus works.

We had artists approaching us, we drifted about, asked questions, visited studios, were surprised, extended invitations. And we asked everyone involved to develop, design, adapt or build "a little piece of Bauhaus" for our wall.

What all the artists have in common is that they consider themselves influenced by the Bauhaus, sometimes more, sometimes less, or that they identify and deal with individual Bauhaus artists, sometimes more, sometimes less directly.

A LITTLE PIECE OF BAUHAUS

Petra Roggel
Leiterin des Goethe-Institut Chicago

Irmi Maunu-Kocian
Programmkoordinatorin des Goethe-Institut Chicago

Unsere Ausstellungsreihe, die wir A Little Piece of Bauhaus *genannt haben, fand zwischen Mai 2016 und Dezember 2018 im Goethe-Institut Chicago statt. Die Idee war, die beiden Bauhausjubiläen durch eine Reihe von Ausstellungen in dieser Zeit zu verbinden: 80 Jahre Chicago Bauhaus 2017 und 100 Jahre Bauhaus in Deutschland 2019. Mit unserer überschaubaren Ausstellungsfläche waren wir konkurrenzlos zu den großen Institutionen in der Stadt. In unserem Eingangsbereich, gleich gegenüber der Rezeption, konnten wir den Künstlern eine kleine Wand anbieten. Daher auch der Titel* A Little Piece of Bauhaus, *denn größere Werke hätten hier keinen Platz gehabt.*

*Eine weitere Idee war, diese Ausstellungen zu nutzen, um mit Künstler*innen aus Chicago und aus Deutschland in Kontakt zu kommen und sie in Kontakt mit uns treten zu lassen. Wir wollten wie ein offenes Medium agieren, nicht weit in die Zukunft planen. Zum Beispiel entpuppte sich eine regelmäßig zu uns kommende Besucherin als Künstlerin, die in einem der ältesten Künstlerhäuser auf der Michigan Avenue, im Fine Arts Building – einem Hochhaus noch mit Fahrstuhlführer –, seit vielen Jahren ein Studio besaß und uns eines Tages einfach zu sich einlud. Ihre Arbeiten haben uns sofort an Arbeiten des Bauhauses erinnert.*

*Für unser Projekt haben wir Künstler*innen auf uns zukommen, haben uns treiben lassen, haben nachgefragt, haben Studios besucht, haben uns überraschen lassen, haben auch selbst eingeladen. Und alle Beteiligten haben wir gebeten, für unsere Wand „ein kleines Stück Bauhaus" zu entwickeln, zu entwerfen, anzupassen oder zu bauen.*

The exhibitions each lasted about three months, parallel to our semesters for German courses at the institute. We then changed them over at the same time as the beginning of the new language courses, invited students and other guests to officially open the new exhibition together with our team, and almost always we were able to get the artists to come in for these moments to give a small introduction and to be available for questions.

Over the course of 2017 we came up with the idea of the residency. One day an artist from Germany unexpectedly turned up at the reception desk with a thick book under her arm. The thick book turned out to be her final thesis, written during a guest semester at the University of Illinois at Chicago. It was a typographic approach to the city of Chicago. The book was like love at first sight to us, and when the artist mentioned she would design it quite differently today, we invited her to come to us and to continue experimenting with it in the summer of 2017.

Since then, we've been able to transform a beautiful glass classroom into an artist's residence in the summer. The residents become part of our team and the students get insights into the creation of a work of art.

We presented the last artist in our exhibition series at the end of 2018. This artist had emigrated from Berlin to Chicago in the 1960s, studied at the SAIC, lived on an island in Lake Michigan and campaigned for environmental protection. All the while she retained her "Berlin lip;" she can still roll off the Berlin dialect today and might soon, after more than half a century, work again in Berlin.

We wanted to conclude our small contribution just in time for the beginning of the major celebration 100 Years of Bauhaus.

Looking back on these ten wonderful works, we noticed that something was missing, namely the moment connecting the artists among themselves. We wanted to tell the story of how we had found each other, and we wanted to tell the stories of the artists. So we decided on a final

*Allen Künstler*innen gemeinsam ist, dass sie sich mal mehr, mal weniger vom Bauhaus beeinflusst sehen oder dass sie sich mal mehr, mal weniger direkt mit einzelnen Künstler*innen des Bauhauses identifizieren und auseinandersetzen.*

*Die Ausstellungen jeweils dauerten ungefähr drei Monate, parallel zu unseren Semestern für die Deutschkurse am Institut. Gewechselt haben wir dann zeitgleich mit dem Beginn der neuen Sprachkurse, haben Kursteilnehmer*innen und andere Gäste eingeladen, zusammen mit unserem Team die jeweils neue Ausstellung offiziell zu eröffnen, und fast immer konnten wir die Künstler*innen für diese Momente gewinnen, eine kleine Einführung zu geben und für Fragen zur Verfügung zu stehen.*

Im Lauf des Jahres 2017 kam uns dann die Idee der Residenz: Eines Tages stand eine Künstlerin aus Deutschland unerwartet mit einem dicken Buch unter dem Arm an der Rezeption. Das dicke Buch entpuppte sich als ihre damalige Abschlussarbeit, die während eines Gastsemesters an der University of Illinois at Chicago entstanden war – es war der Versuch einer Typografie der Stadt Chicago. Das Buch war für uns wie eine Liebe auf den ersten Blick, und als die Künstlerin meinte, sie würde es heutzutage ganz anders gestalten, luden wir sie im Sommer 2017 zu uns ein, daran weiter zu experimentieren.

*Seitdem können wir im Sommer einen schönen gläsernen Klassenraum in eine Künstlerresidenz umwandeln. Die Resident*innen werden Teil unseres Teams und die Kursteilnehmer*innen erhalten Einblicke in das Entstehen einer künstlerischen Arbeit.*

Ende 2018 präsentierten wir die letzte Künstlerin in unserer Ausstellungsreihe. Diese Künstlerin war in den 1960er-Jahren von Berlin nach Chicago ausgewandert, hatte an der SAIC studiert, auf einer Insel im Michigansee gelebt und dort für den Umweltschutz gekämpft – dabei hat sie ihre Berliner Schnauze beibehalten, kann heute noch „berlinern" und wird vielleicht bald wieder, nach mehr als einem halben Jahrhundert, in Berlin arbeiten.

"little piece of Bauhaus." This contribution is the design of a book. It will tell the stories, it will connect the artists and it will tell of the openness with which we all like to experiment.

Our biggest thanks go to the nine artists. Their willingness and commitment to exhibit on our little wall has touched us deeply and we are very proud!

We also wish to thank the three authors who looked at our exhibition, the city of Chicago and the Bauhaus ideas from the perspective of architecture, photography, design, collaboration, and movement.

We thank mischen, our designers Harri and Vera, for this publication. They encouraged us to believe in our stories. We would also like to thank Kerber Verlag for publishing support.

And we thank Douglas Clonch, without whom art would never have gotten on our wall, for his dedication in implementing and adapting the artistic ideas.

Pünktlich zum Beginn der großen Feierlichkeiten 100 Jahre Bauhaus wollten wir abschließen mit unserem kleinen Beitrag.

Beim Rückblick auf diese zehn wunderbaren Künstler*innen fiel uns auf, dass noch etwas fehlte. Es fehlte das verbindende Moment der Künstler*innen untereinander. Wir wollten die Geschichte erzählen, wie wir zueinander gefunden hatten, und wir wollten die Geschichten der Künstler*innen erzählen. Und so entschieden wir uns für ein abschließendes „kleines Stück Bauhaus". Dieser Beitrag ist die Gestaltung eines Buches. Es wird die Geschichten erzählen, es wird die Künstler untereinander verbinden und es wird von der Offenheit erzählen, mit der wir alle so gerne experimentieren.

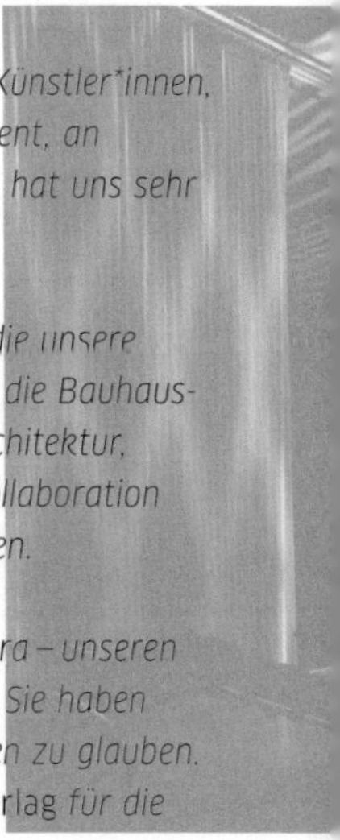

Unser größter Dank gilt den neun Künstler*innen, ihre Bereitschaft und ihr Engagement, an unserer kleinen Wand auszustellen, hat uns sehr berührt und stolz gemacht!

Wir danken den drei Autor*innen, die unsere Ausstellung, die Stadt Chicago und die Bauhausideen aus den Perspektiven der Architektur, der Fotografie, des Designs, der Kollaboration und der Bewegung betrachtet haben.

Wir danken mischen, Harri und Vera – unseren Gestaltern –, für diese Publikation. Sie haben uns ermutigt, an unsere Geschichten zu glauben. Ebenso danken wir dem Kerber Verlag für die verlegerische Betreuung.

Und wir danken Douglas Clonch, ohne den die Kunst nie an unsere Wand gelangt wäre, für seinen Einsatz beim Umsetzen und Anpassen der künstlerischen Ideen.

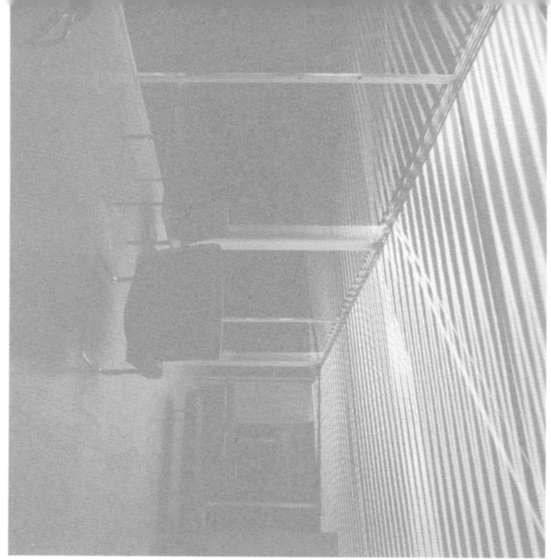

FLOW/Im Fluss *was the name of the first jointly produced spectacular light and water installation by Luftwerk and the Goethe-Institut. The pictures from this work – produced as part of the twentieth anniversary of the sister-city program between Hamburg and Chicago – were so overwhelmingly beautiful that the Goethe-Institut Head Office chose them for our Christmas cards, which were sent around the world.*

FLOW/Im Fluss *hieß die erste gemeinsam produzierte, spektakuläre Licht- und Wasserinstallation von Luftwerk und dem Goethe-Institut. Die Bilder dieser im Rahmen der 20-jährigen Städtepartnerschaft zwischen Hamburg und Chicago entstandenen Arbeit waren so überwältigend schön, dass die Zentrale des Goethe-Instituts sie als Motiv für unsere weltweit versendeten Weihnachtskarten auswählte.*

LUFTWERK
INSITE

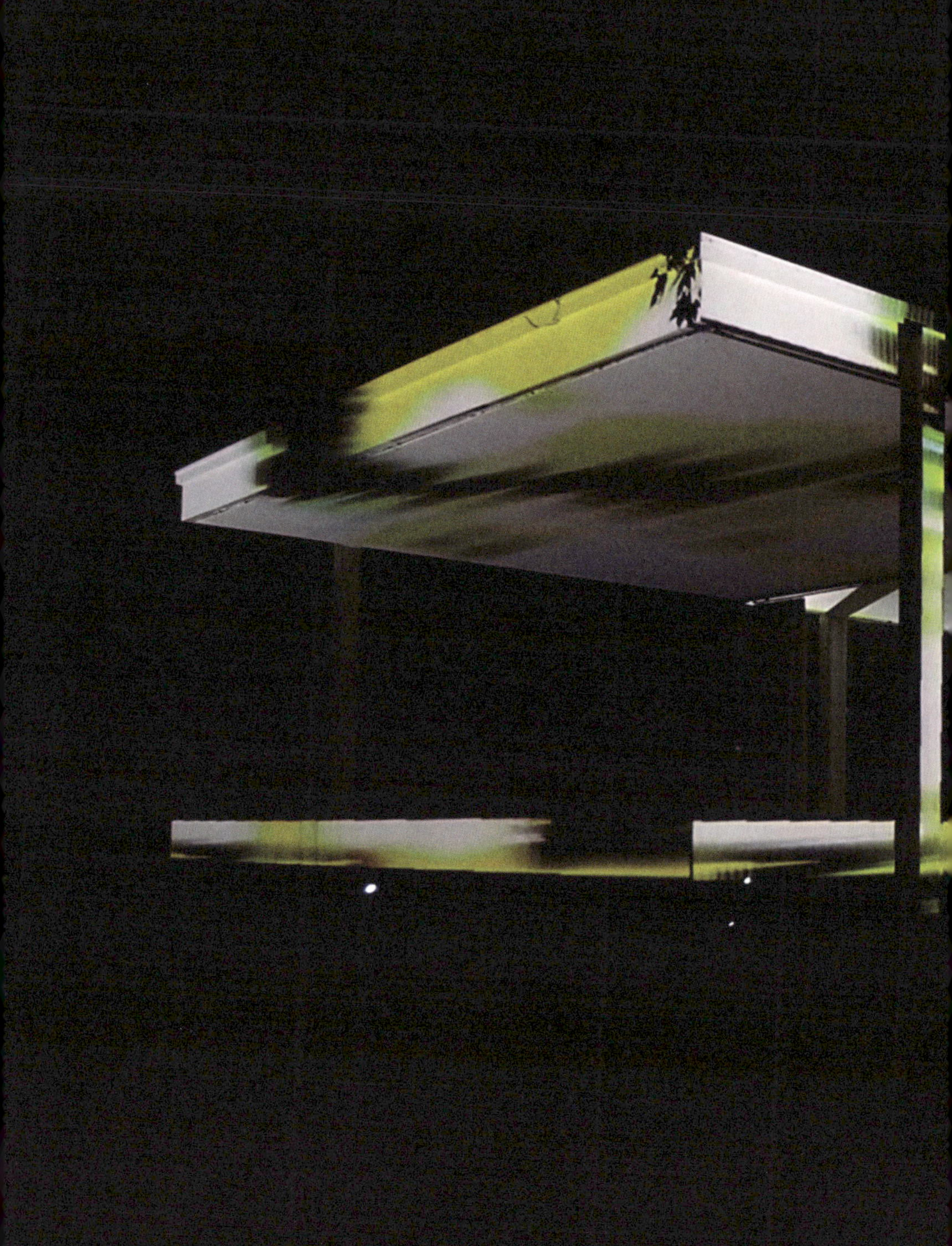

INsite, 2014
Pp. 14–21

INsite, 2014
S. 14–21

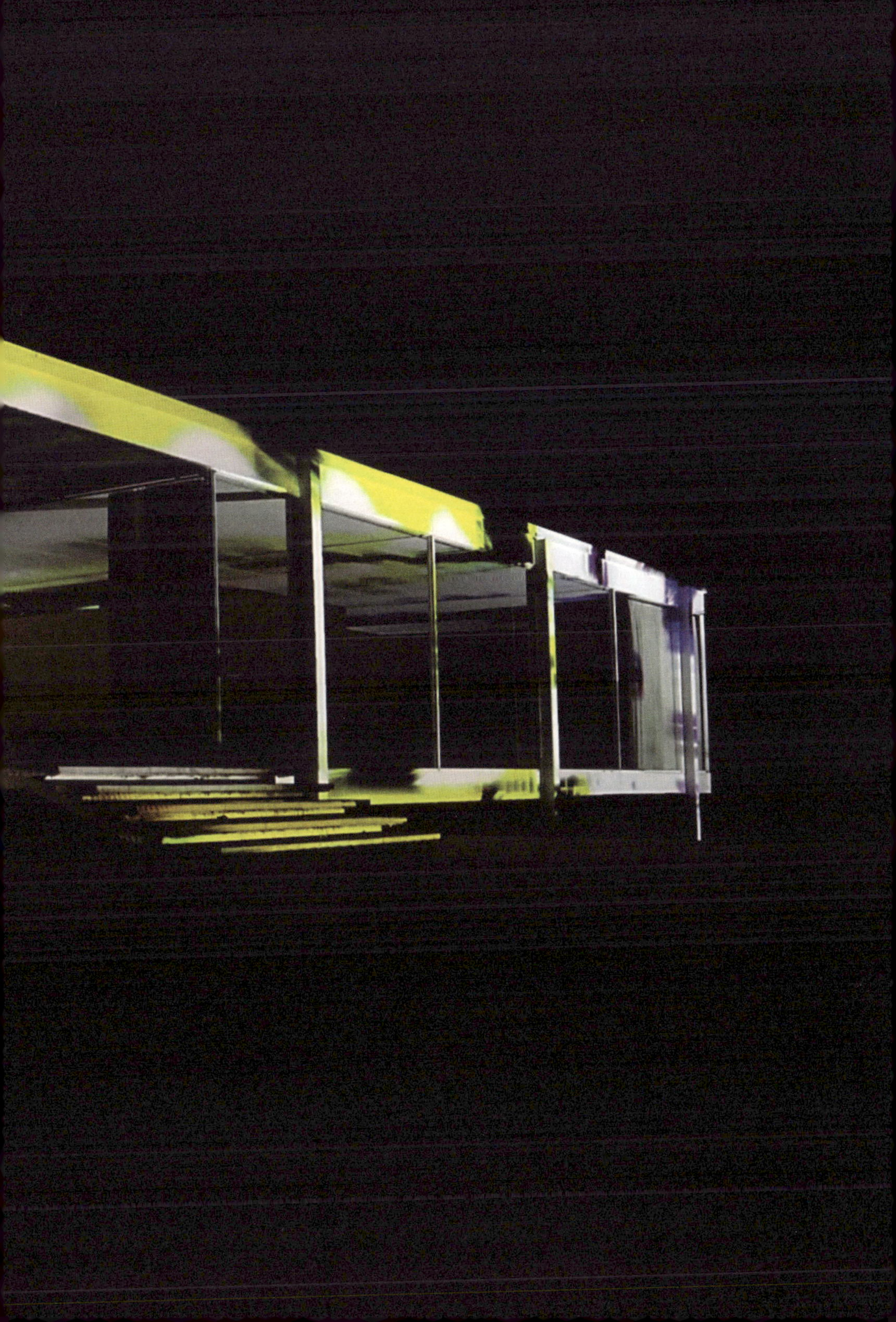

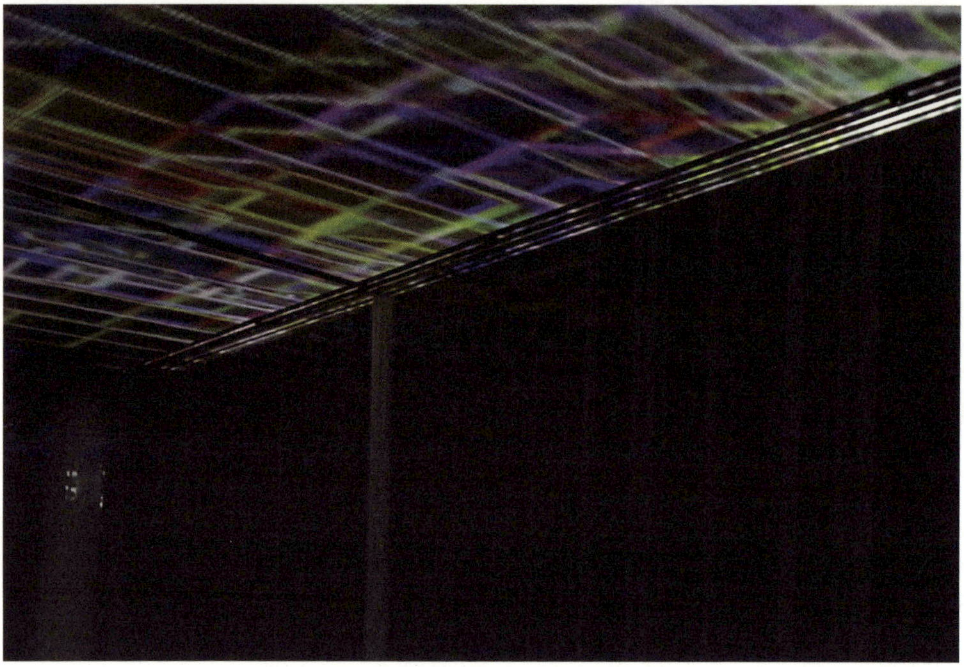

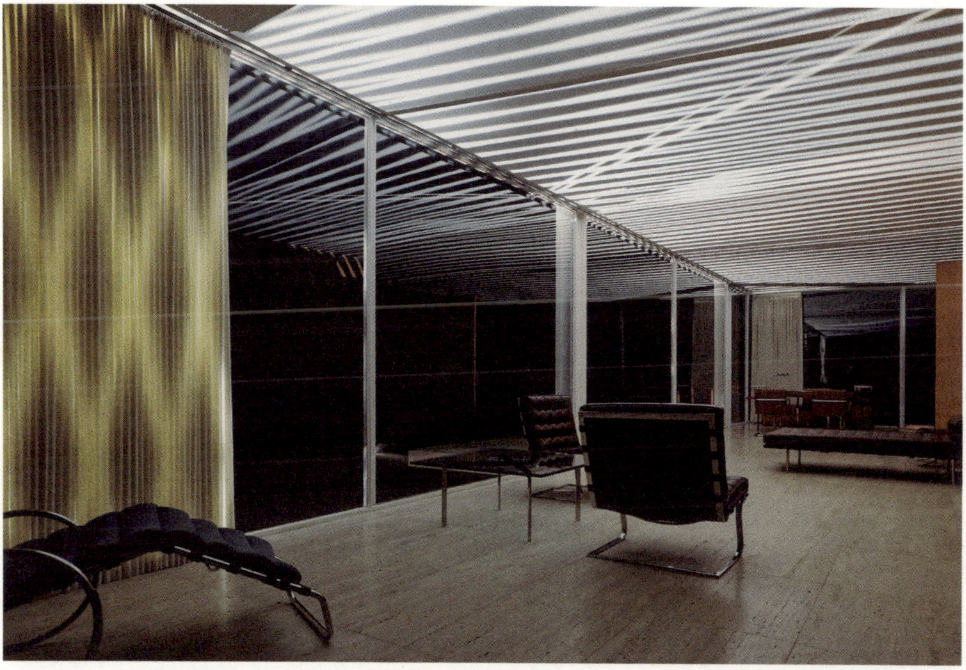

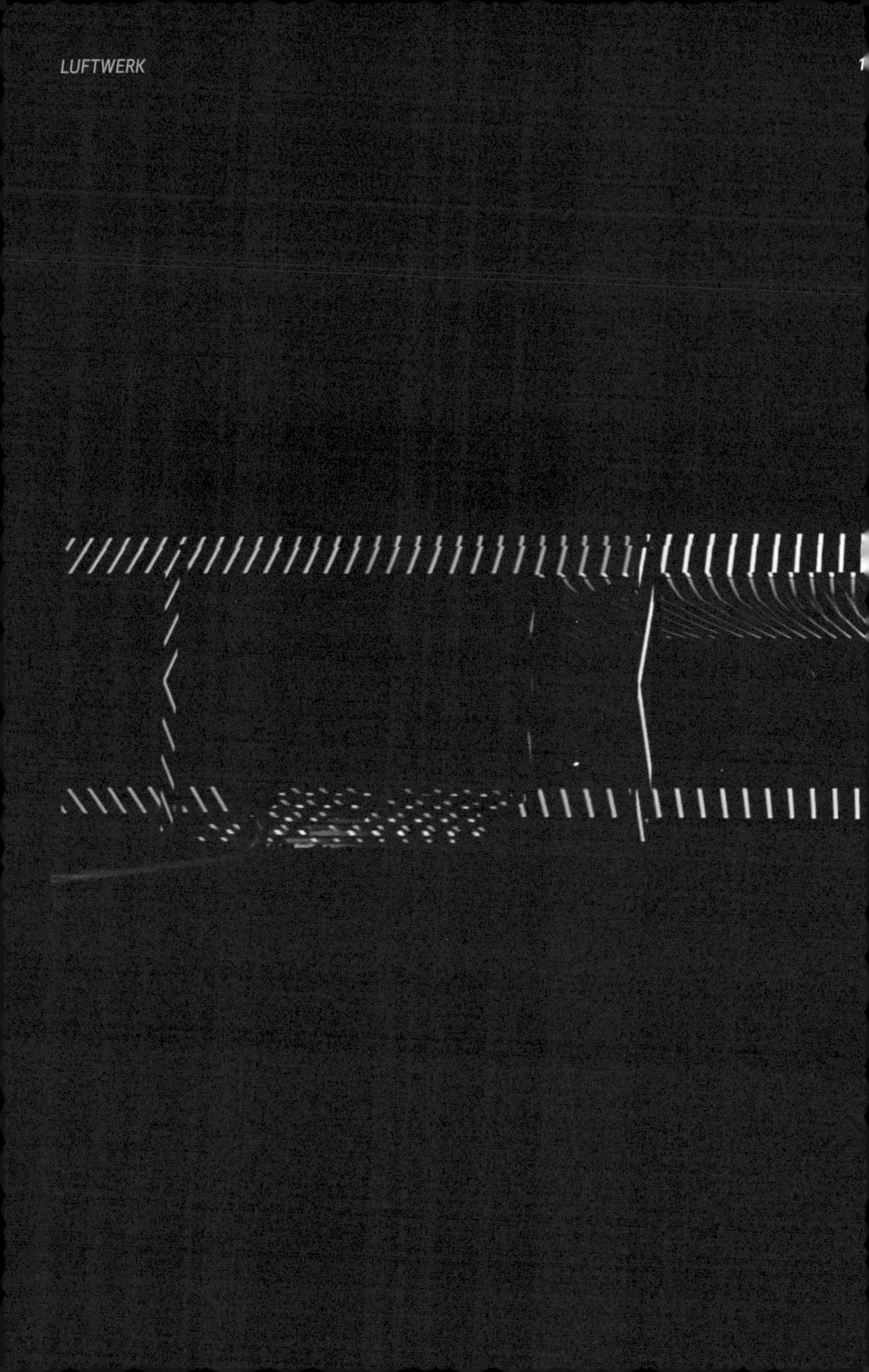

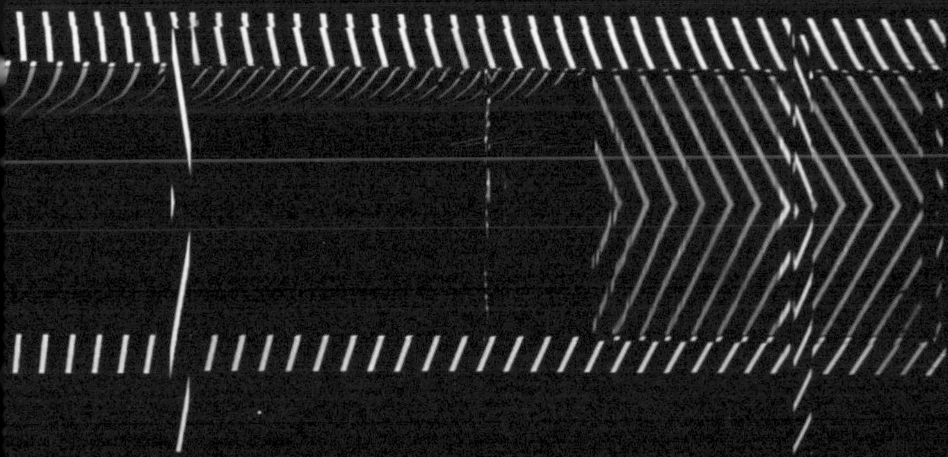

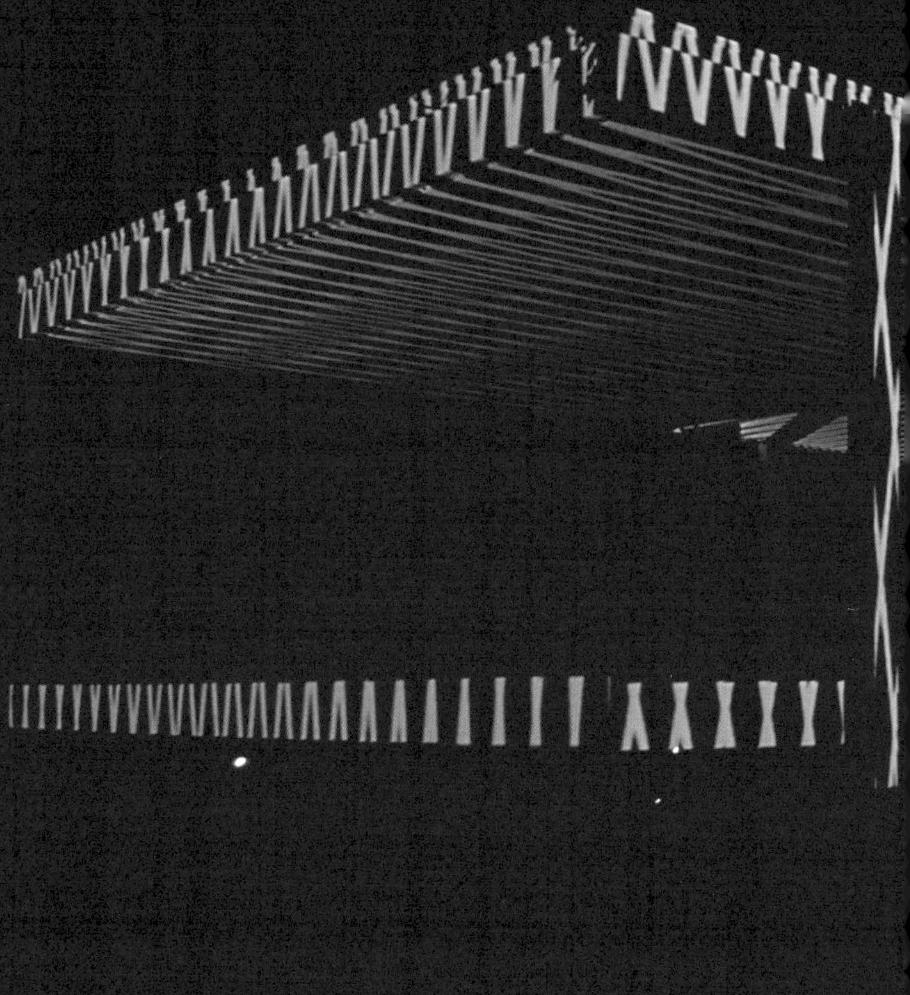

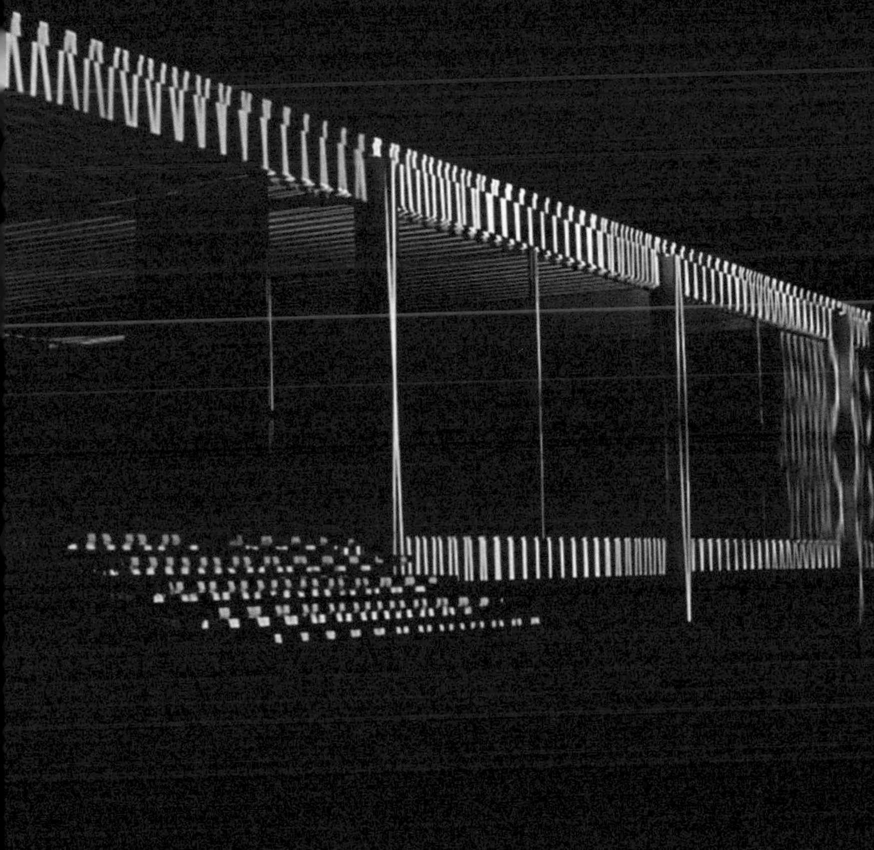

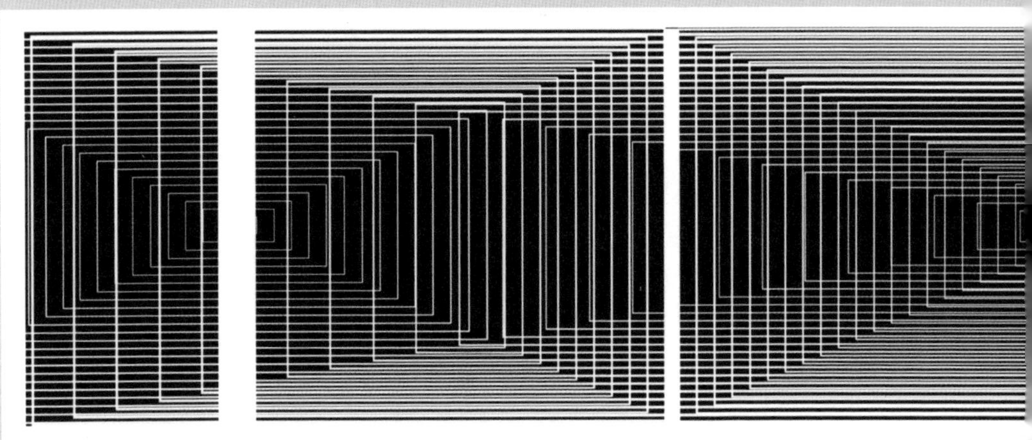

INsite, 2015
Digital print, shadow box
Frame 27 × 65 inches

INsite, 2015
Digitaldruck, Schattenrahmen
Rahmen 27 × 65 Zoll

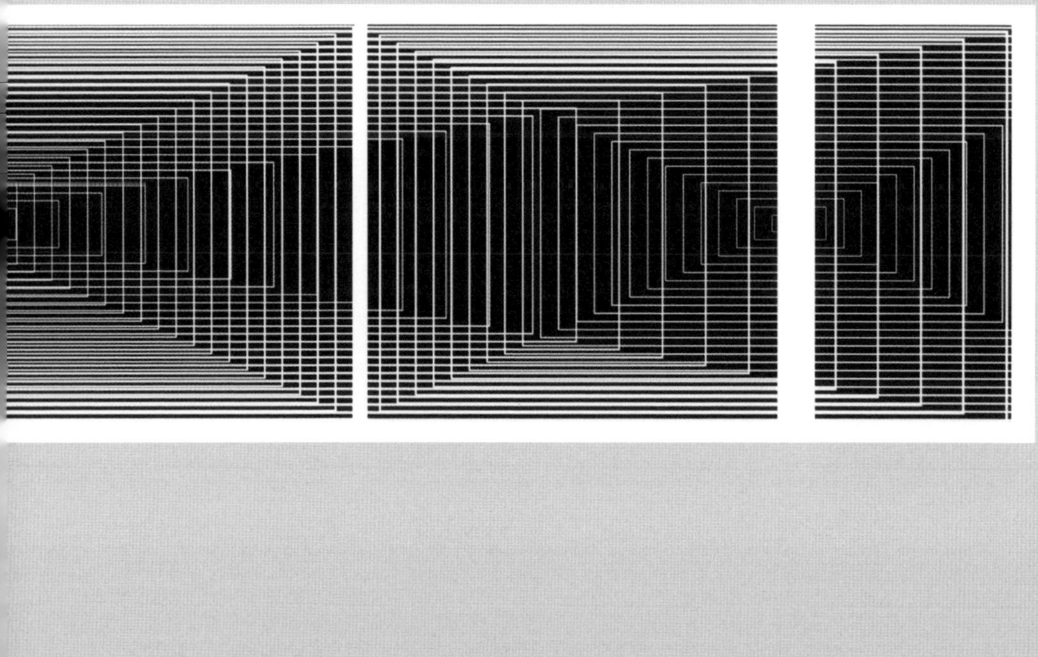

WHAT DO YOU DO WITH A REVERED MASTERPIECE OF THE 20TH CENTURY?

Steve Dietz
President and Artistic Director,
Northern Lights, Minneapolis

INsite *is a looping composition divided into three sections roughly corresponding to the structure of the house, the fluidity of its transparent glass walls, and the organic, where nature meets geometry. Luftwerk uses precision projection mapping, especially in the first movement, to highlight the horizontal structural steel beams that enable the glass walls to enclose the volume of the space with such an ethereal mass. Subsequent projections of abstracted patterns are like an artist's MRI of the interior volume of Farnsworth, flooding it with images of fluidity created in their studio in a playful but systematic topographic investigation. In the last movement, color enters in and nature is projected within the volume of the house. Dappled sensory memories from the daytime meld with the structural outline of the house, transforming it.*

In a sense, there are two Farnsworth Houses. There is the one that most people get to experience during the day, and there is Farnsworth at night. During the day, Farnsworth hovers above the grassy landscape and the glass walls provide a transparent view that is also subtly hermetic. Even though there is no visual barrier, interior and exterior are sealed off from one another. You are in nature, but not necessarily 'amongst' it.

At night, Luftwerk's projections literalize the hovering quality of the structure, highlighting the horizontal steel beams supporting the house but virtually eliminating, through the absence of illumination, any connection to the ground. The house becomes unmoored. From the inside there is an epidermal transformation. The glass skin becomes reflective and the space expands fractally toward the indefinite. But beyond

WAS MACHT MAN MIT EINEM VEREHRTEN MEISTERWERK DES 20. JAHRHUNDERTS?

Steve Dietz
Präsident und Künstlerischer Leiter
von Northern Lights, Minneapolis

INsite *ist eine loopartige Komposition, die sich in drei Teile gliedert, die auf die Struktur des Hauses, die Fluidität seiner transparenten Glaswände und das organische Aufeinandertreffen von Natur und Geometrie anspielen. Vor allem im ersten Teil nutzt Luftwerk präzises Projektionsmapping zur Betonung der horizontalen Stahlträger. So entsteht der Eindruck, dass die Glaswände das Rauminnere auf äußerst ätherische Weise umschließen. Die anschließende Projektion abstrakter Muster erinnert an ein künstlerisches MRT vom Innenraum des Farnsworth House. Es wird von Bildern der Fluidität durchströmt, die in einer spielerischen, aber systematischen topografischen Untersuchung im Studio erstellt wurden. Im letzten Teil kommt Farbe ins Spiel und die Natur wird ins Hausinnere projiziert. Bruchstückhafte Sinneserinnerungen des Tages verschmelzen mit den strukturellen Umrissen des Hauses und verwandeln es dadurch.*

Auf gewisse Weise gibt es zwei Farnsworth Häuser. Einerseits jenes, das die meisten Menschen am Tag erleben, andererseits Farnsworth bei Nacht. Am Tag schwebt Farnsworth über dem Rasengelände und die Glaswände bieten einen transparenten, gleichwohl subtil hermetischen Ausblick. Obwohl dem Blick nichts im Wege steht, sind Innen und Außen voneinander isoliert. Man ist in der Natur, aber nicht direkt „mittendrin".

Bei Nacht wird durch die Projektionen von Luftwerk der schwebende Charakter des Baus herausgearbeitet. Die horizontalen Stahlträger, die das Haus stützen, werden hervorgehoben, während die Verbindung zum Boden durch die fehlende Beleuchtung praktisch aufgelöst wird. Das Haus verliert die Bodenhaftung. Aus dem Inneren heraus findet eine epidermale Verwandlung statt.

the glow of refracted light there is no landscape, no nature, only a primeval dark.

There is one other critical element to Luftwerk's illuminating exploration of the philosophy of Mies, and it is the musical score of Owen Clay Condon. Condon uses a number of different instruments in his own sonic exploration of Farnsworth, but the key is his use of B as the resonant frequency of the physical distance between floor and ceiling – the height of the volume of Farnsworth. It is a sonification of the structure, which melds minimalist percussion with the otherworldly tones of a vibraphone to encourage a reverie of Farnsworth where past and present and future meet in a kaleidoscope of light and sound and remembrance and imagination.

Auf der Glashaut werden Reflektionen sichtbar und der Raum weitet sich fraktal ins Unendliche aus. Doch hinter dem Schein des gebrochenen Lichts gibt es keine Landschaft, keine Natur, nur urzeitliche Dunkelheit.

Ein weiteres Element prägt die Illumination, mit der Luftwerk die Philosophie Mies van der Rohes erforscht: die musikalische Untermalung von Owen Clay Condon. Condon setzt in seiner eigenen klanglichen Erkundung des Farnsworth House verschiedene Instrumente ein. Eine entscheidende Rolle spielt der Ton h als Widerhall des physischen Abstands zwischen Boden und Decke – der Raumhöhe des Farnsworth House. Es ergibt sich eine Verklanglichung des Baukörpers, die minimalistische perkussive Mittel mit den jenseitigen Tönen des Vibraphons verbindet, so dass eine Träumerei über Farnsworth entsteht, welche Vergangenheit, Gegenwart und Zukunft in einem Kaleidoskop aus Licht und Klang, Erinnerung und Fantasie aufeinandertreffen lässt.

The work of Assaf Evron recently received remarkable attention, also through A Little Piece of Bauhaus. *Since his two exhibitions at the Goethe-Institut, he has shown his work in several galleries in Chicago and New York. The windows to the art world seem to have opened.*

Die Arbeit von Assaf Evron erhielt auch durch A Little Piece of Bauhaus *eine bemerkenswerte Aufmerksamkeit. Seit seinen beiden Ausstellungen im Goethe-Institut zeigte er seine Werke in Galerien in Chicago und New York. Die Fenster zur Kunstwelt scheinen sich geöffnet zu haben.*

ASSAF EVRON
MIES WINDOWS – CROWN HALL, CHICAGO

Untitled (S.R. Crown Hall), 2017
Pigment print / aluminum
Frame 50 × 40 inches each

Untitled (S.R. Crown Hall), 2017
Pigmentdruck / Aluminum
Jeder Rahmen 50 × 40 Zoll

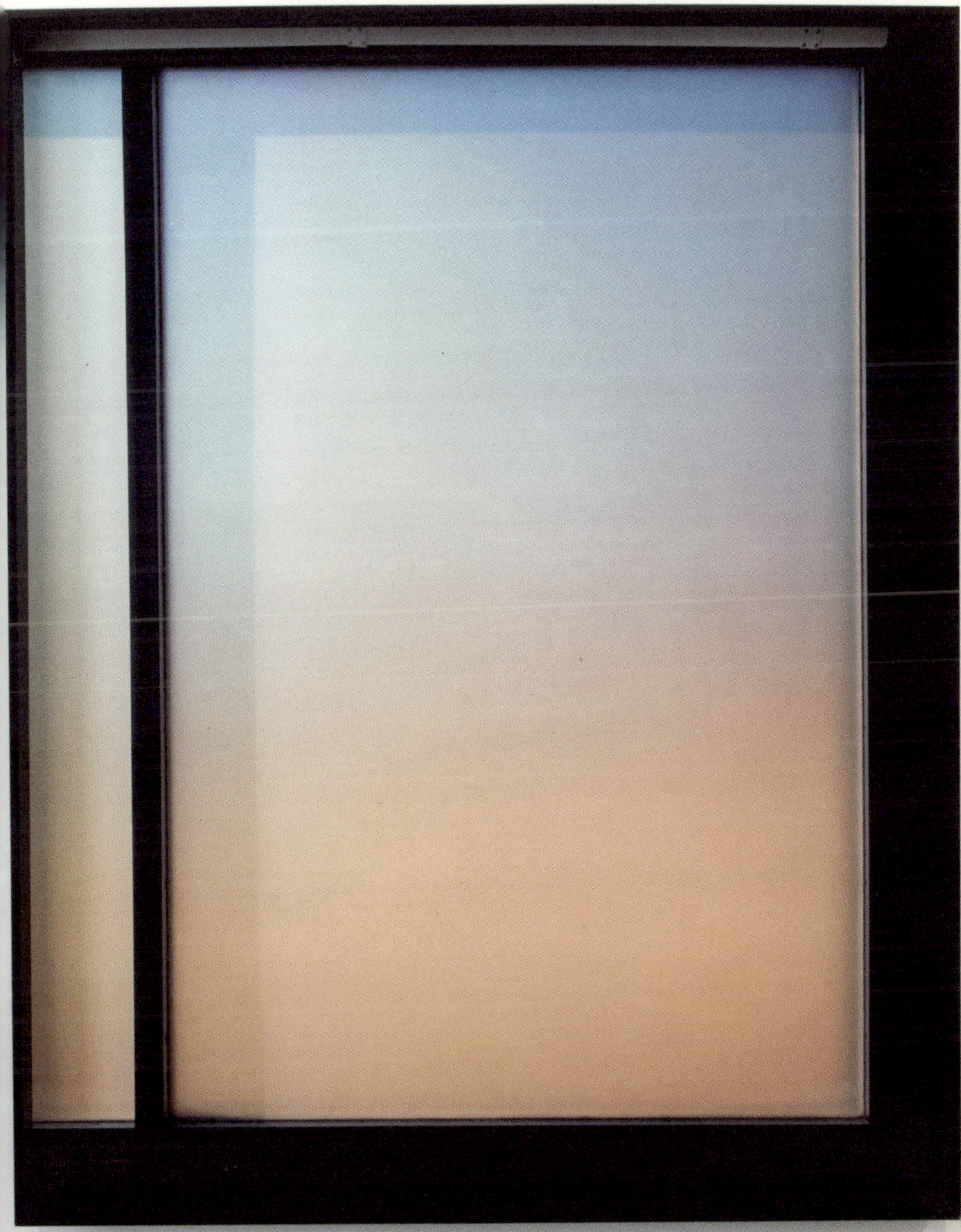

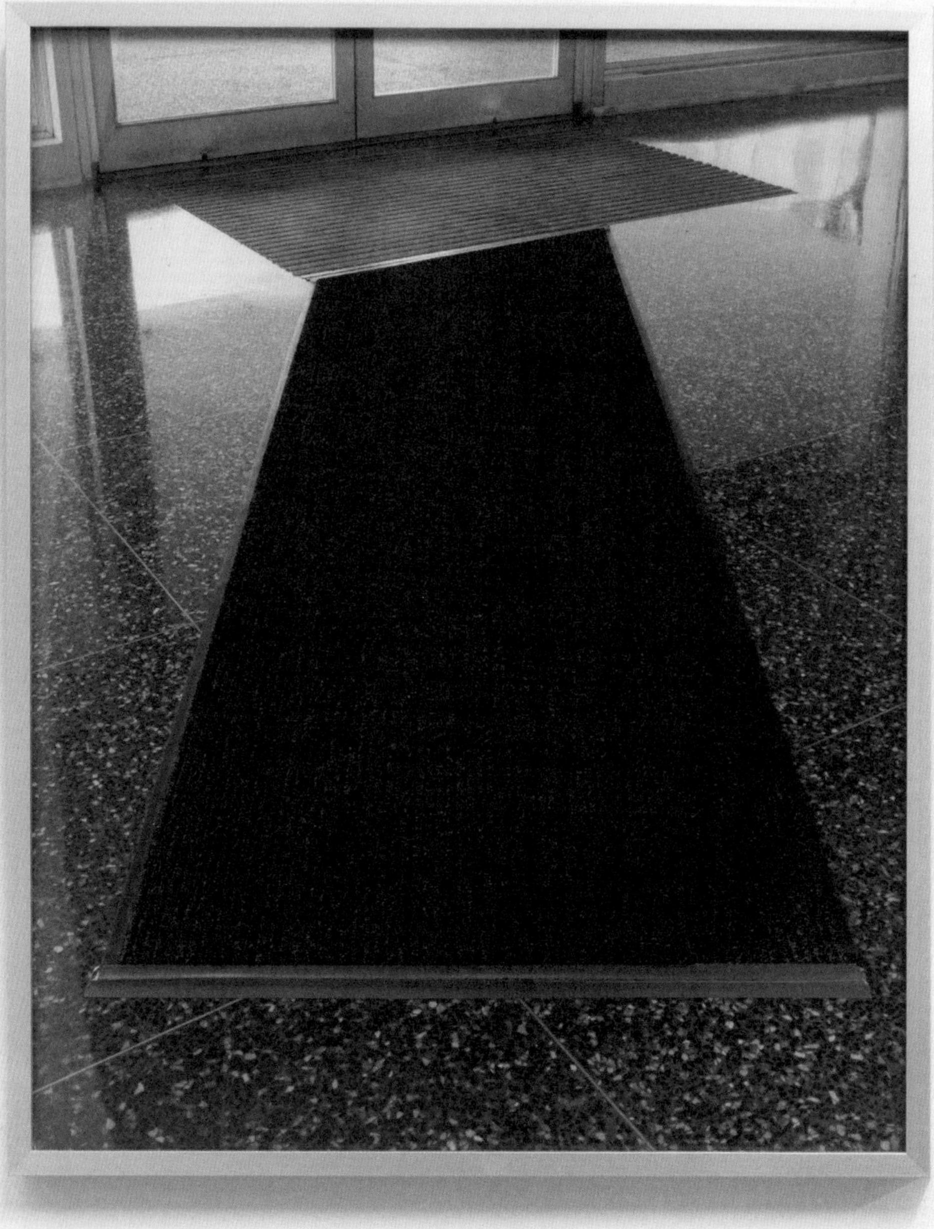

Untitled (2400 Lakeview), 2013
Pigment print / aluminum
Frame 20 × 16 inches each

Untitled (2400 Lakeview), 2013
Pigmentdruck / Aluminum
Jeder Rahmen 20 × 16 Zoll

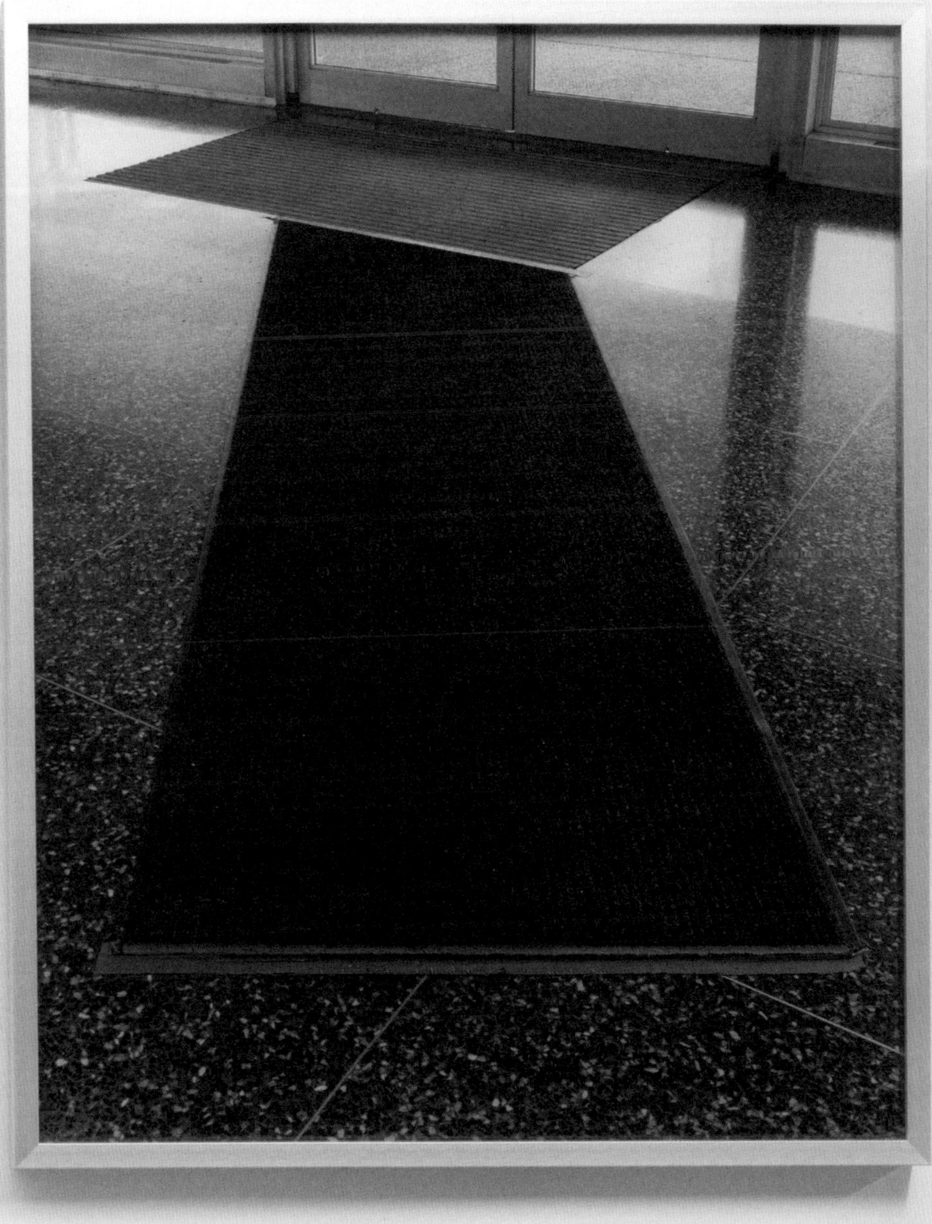

MIES WINDOWS

Andrei Pop
Professor of Art History and Committee on Social Thought, University of Chicago

It is a simple, spare object: showing a clean, well-lit place. An aluminum frame cradles two color photographs in the same large format, showing two window panes bookended by their black metal frames. The sash in the center may be the same – if these are panes of the same window. Above both – if they are one window frame – hangs a white plastic blind cover. The object looks like a puzzle. And a glance at the title reveals that we were right – these are windows – but puzzling ones. For these are windows in the S.R. Crown Hall at the Illinois Institute of Technology, designed by Mies van der Rohe. Where in that lateral monolith are such intimate windows to be found? The façade has three registers of windows–monumental upper ones, the man-sized middle windows, and the half-sized bottom windows, which are below the raised floor of the main space, basement windows really. Evron captured what looks like a sunset gradient in them: turquois gradually turning to the unlikeliest shade of orangy pink. Why don't trees and buildings and the feet of pedestrians intrude? They are frosted windows, which refract the light. It needn't be sunset. And so the object remains a puzzle. Of what it shows, I say what I first said of the artwork: The window is a simple, discreet object: the world a clean, well-lit place.

MIES' FENSTER

Andrei Pop
Professor für Kunstgeschichte und Mitglied des Committee on Social Thought, University of Chicago

Es ist ein einfaches, schlichtes Objekt: Es zeigt eine ebenmäßige, gut ausgeleuchtete Fläche. Ein Aluminiumrahmen fasst zwei Farbfotografien in gleich großem Format, sie zeigen zwei Fensterelemente mit schwarzen Metallumrandungen. Der mittlere Flügel könnte der gleiche sein – wenn alles zum gleichen Fenster gehört. Über den beiden Elementen befindet sich – so sie ein und dasselbe Fenster bilden – eine weiße Kunststoffjalousie. Das Objekt erinnert an ein Rätselbild. Und ein Blick auf den Titel bestätigt die Annahme, dass hier Fenster dargestellt sind, die uns indes vor ein Rätsel stellen. Denn die Fenster befinden sich in der von Mies van der Rohe entworfenen S.R. Crown Hall des Illinois Institute of Technology. Wo finden sich an diesem Monolithen so beschauliche Fenster? Die Fassade hat drei Fensterausführungen – oben monumental große, in der Mitte mannshohe und unten halbhohe, die souterrainartig unter dem erhöhten Erdgeschoss liegen. Evron hat einen Farbverlauf eingefangen, der an einen Sonnenuntergang erinnert: Türkis, das sich ganz allmählich in einen undefinierbaren orange-roséfarbenen Ton verwandelt. Warum stören hier keine Bäume oder Gebäude oder die Füße vorübergehender Passanten? Die Scheiben, die das Licht reflektieren, sind satiniert. Es muss kein Sonnenuntergang sein. Und so bleibt das Objekt ein Rätsel. Was ich anfangs über das Kunstwerk sagte, sage ich nun über das, was es darstellt: Das Fenster ist ein einfaches, schlichtes Objekt, die Welt ist eine ebenmäßige, gut ausgeleuchtete Fläche.

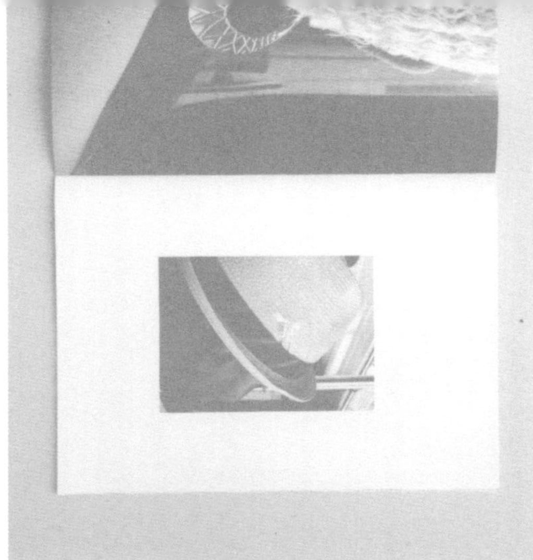

We've never met Rebecca Wilton in person; she was recommended to us as an artist who has focused her work on Detroit for years, long before the hype about the city began. Her photographs of Lafayette Park, the location of residential buildings designed by Ludwig Mies van der Rohe, are brittle and touching portraits of the people who live there.

Rebecca Wilton haben wir bisher nie persönlich getroffen; sie wurde uns als eine Künstlerin empfohlen, die sich schon seit Jahren mit Detroit auseinandersetzt, lange bevor der Hype um diese Stadt begann. Ihre Fotos vom Lafayette Park, in dem die von Ludwig Mies van der Rohe gestalteten Wohnhäuser stehen, sind brüchige und anrührende Porträts der dort lebenden Menschen.

REBECCA WILTON
LA FAYETTE, DETROIT

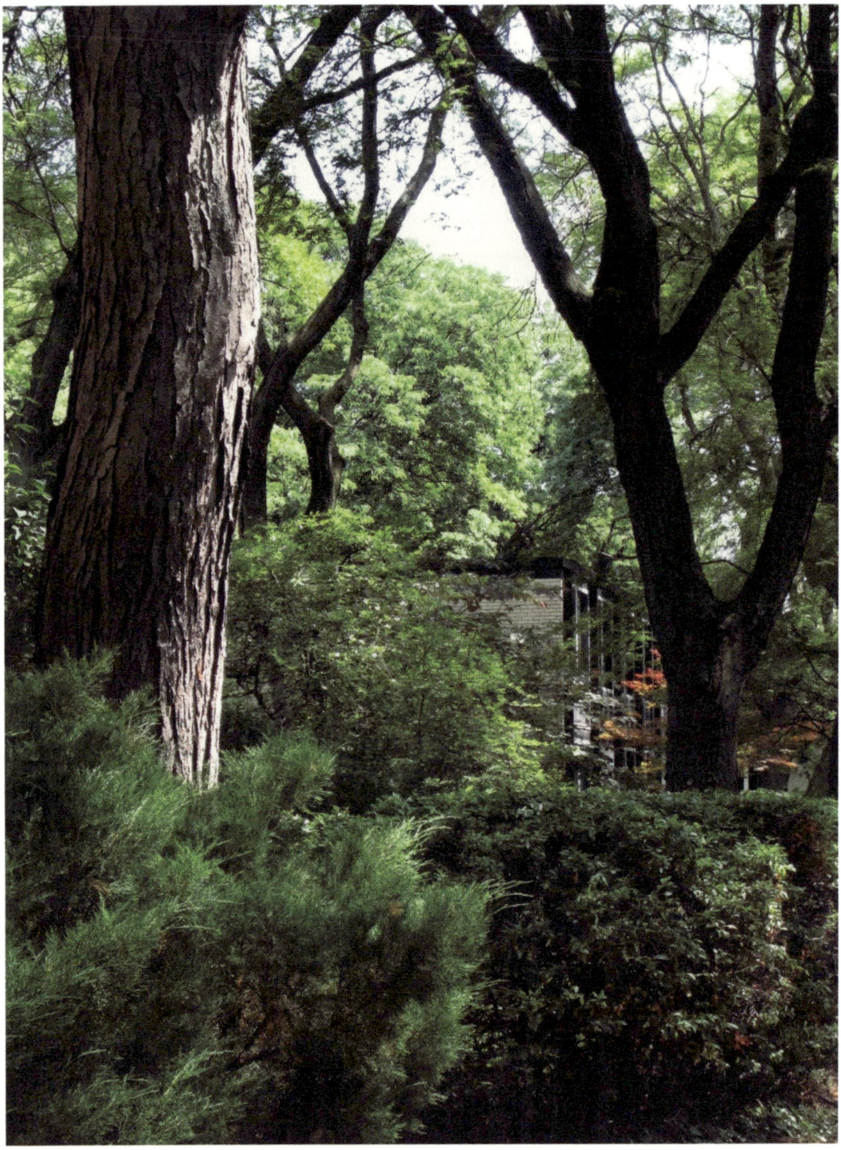

Photographs from
La Fayette, 2014
Self-published, Berlin, 40 pages,
23 color illustrations, 10.2 × 7.7 inches
Pp. 36–42

Fotos aus
La Fayette, 2014
Selbstveröffentlicht, Berlin, 40 Seiten,
23 Farbabbildungen 10,2 × 7,7 Zoll
S. 36–42

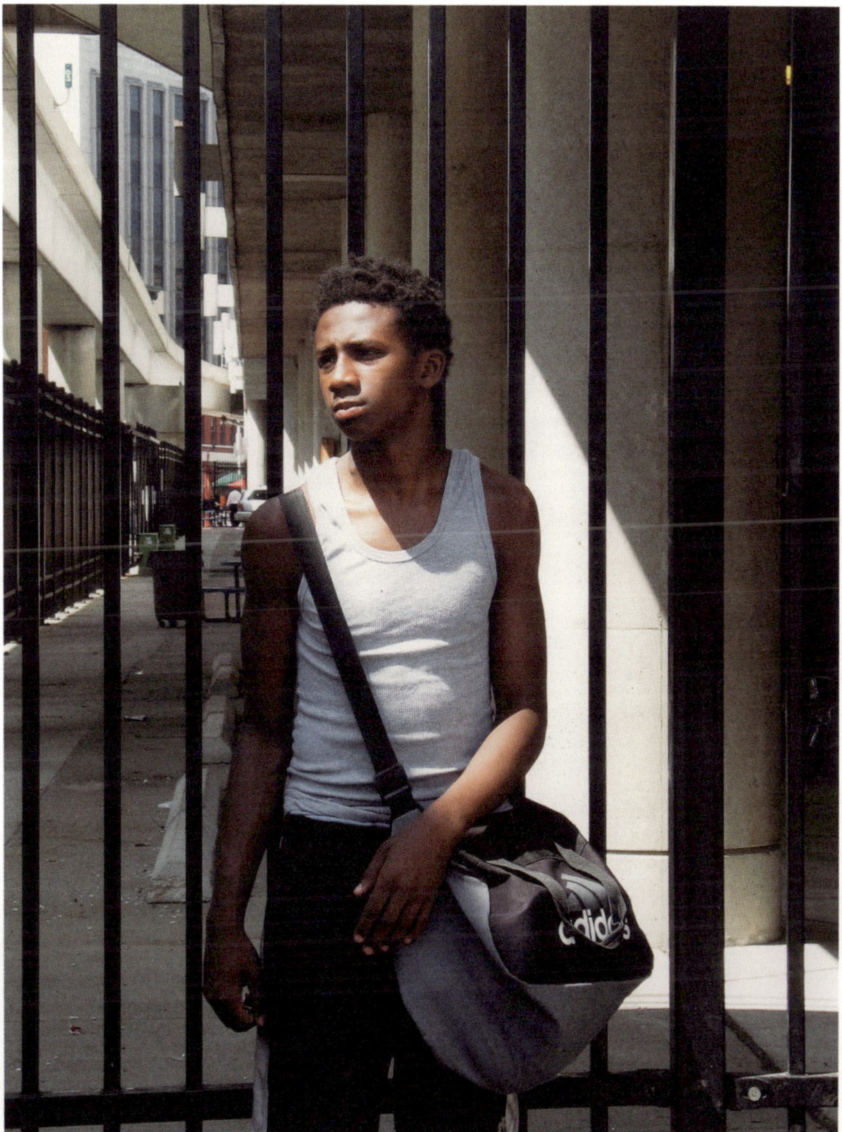
adidas

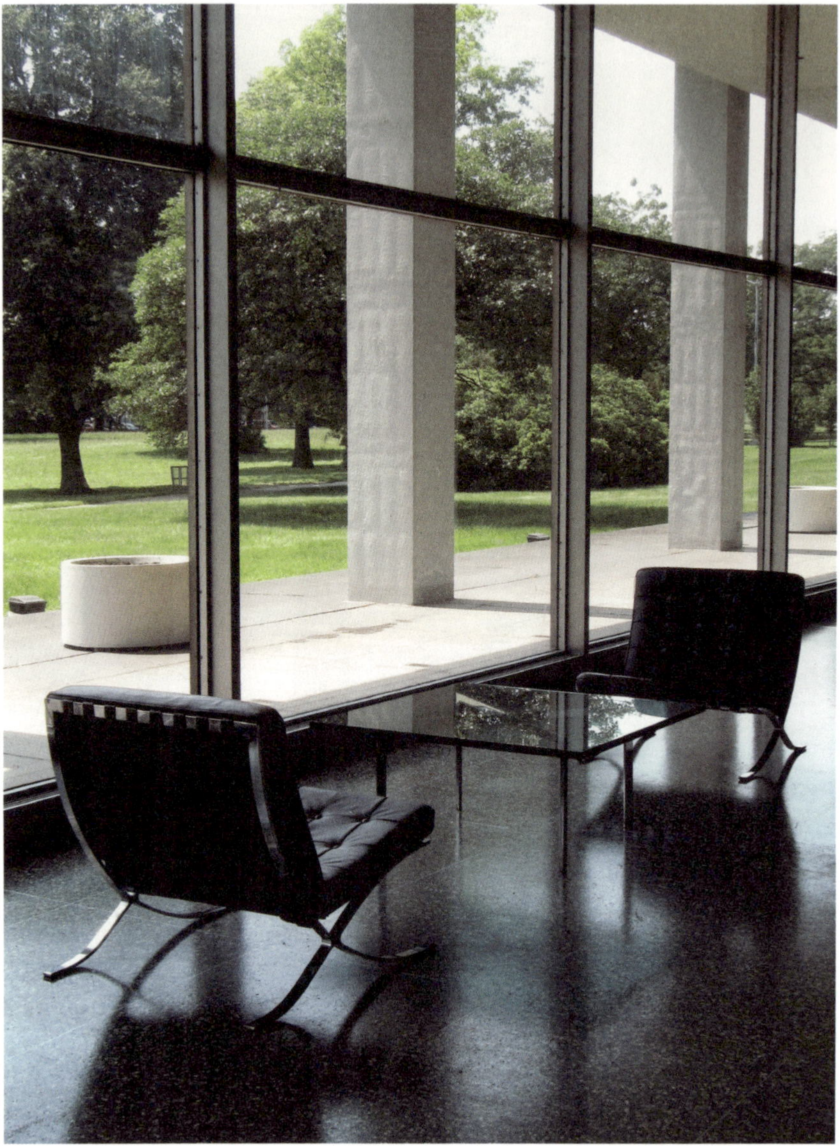

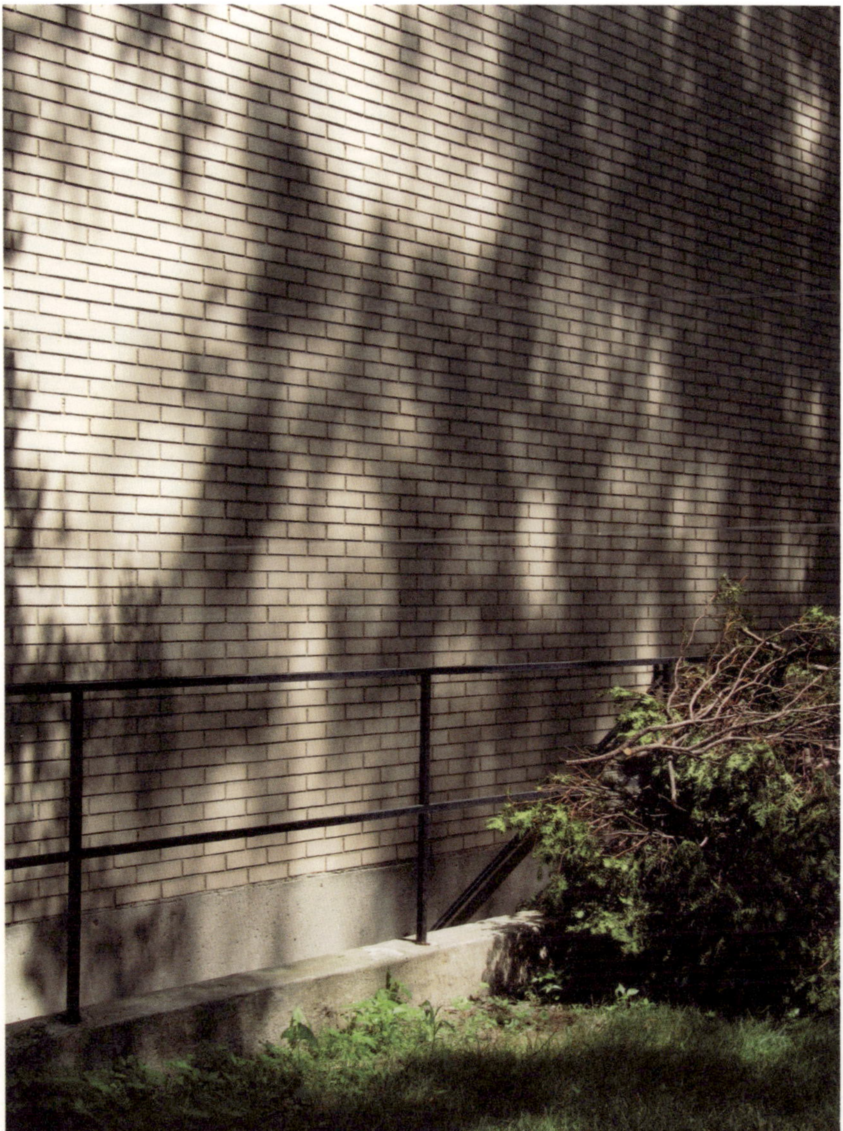

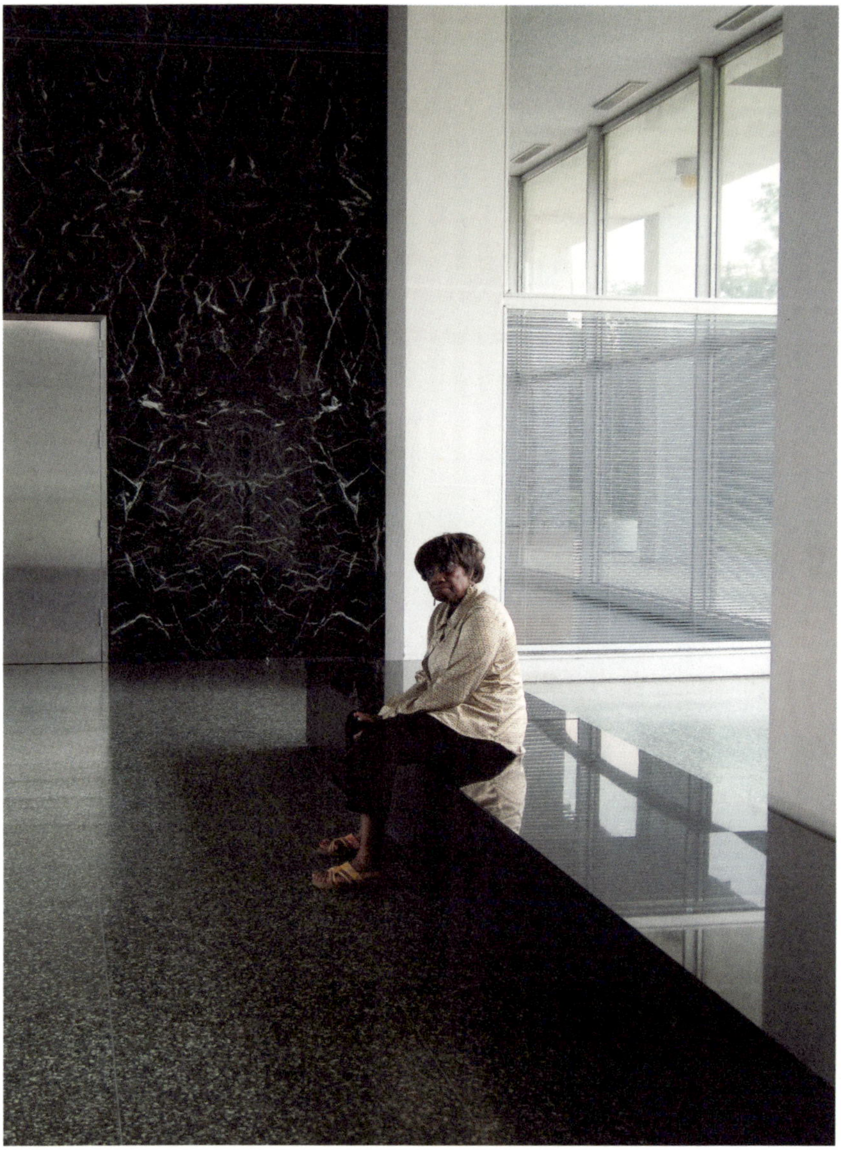

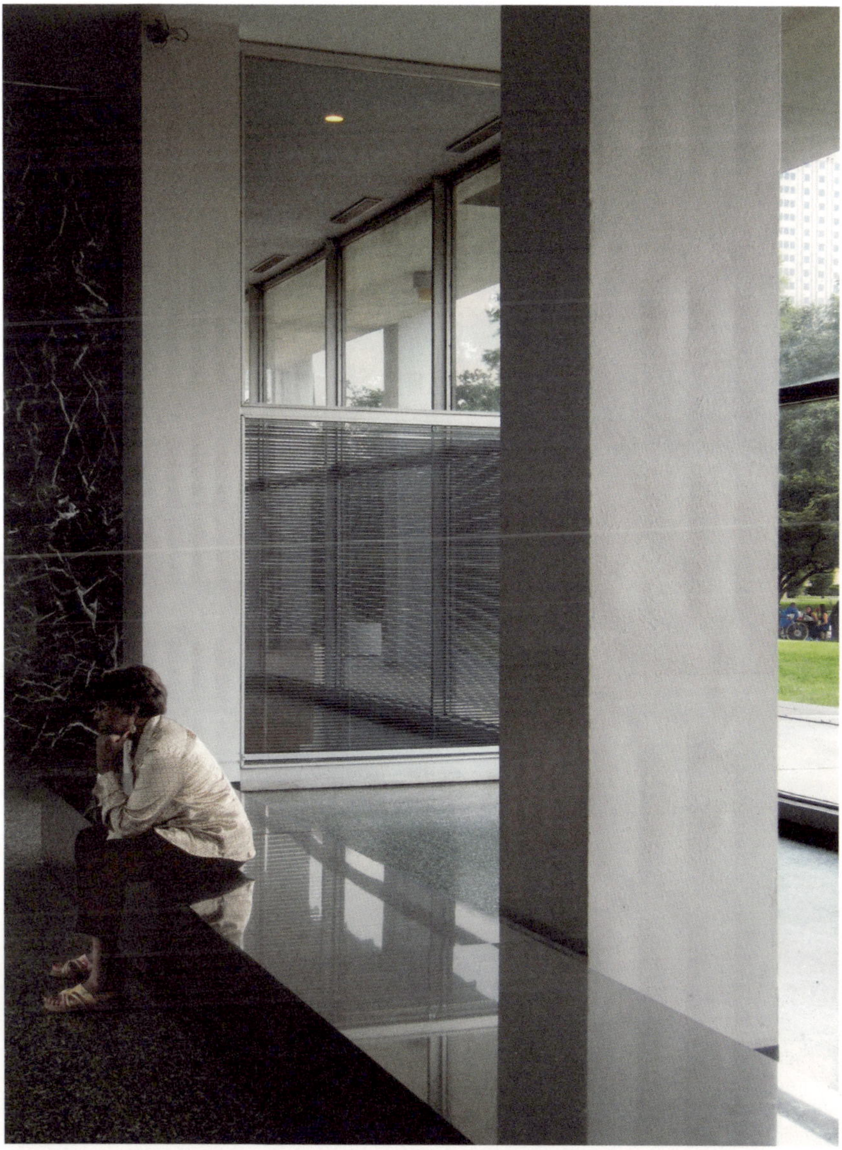

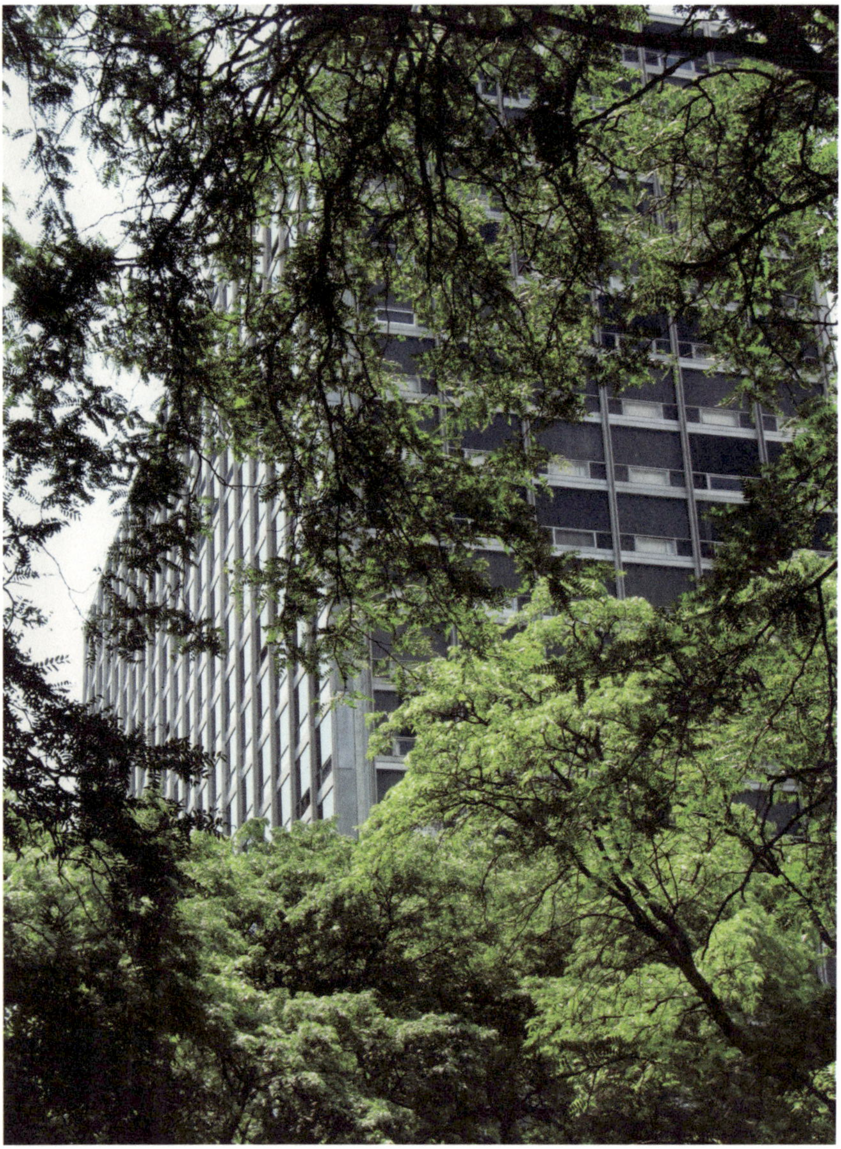

LA FAYETTE

Rebecca Wilton

A central theme in the work of Rebecca Wilton is the detailed presentation of historic overlaps in urban and rural environments as they present themselves in structures, public spaces, and nature.

Her artistic process resembles an archeological dig as she looks for cultural inscriptions at specific locations to be captured through photographic means. In a meticulously chosen pictorial language, she excavates layers of time to reveal a location. This process displays an additional aspect of Rebecca Wilton's work, namely the difference between what is seen and what is known, and how both are layered in a photographic image.

LA FAYETTE

Rebecca Wilton

Ein zentrales Motiv in der Arbeit von Rebecca Wilton ist das Herausarbeiten historischer Überlagerungen in städtischer wie ländlicher Umgebung, die sich in Gebäuden, öffentlichen Plätzen oder in der Natur niederschlagen.

Ihr Arbeitsprozess gleicht dabei einer archäologischen Untersuchung, in der sie die kulturellen Einschreibungen eines Ortes aufspürt und mit fotografischen Mitteln sichtbar macht. In einer sorgfältig gewählten Bildsprache legt sie die Zeitschichten frei, die ein jeder Ort erkennen lässt. Darin wird ein weiterer Aspekt von Rebecca Wiltons Arbeit deutlich: die Differenz zwischen dem Gesehenen und Gewussten, sowie deren Überlagerung im fotografischen Bild.

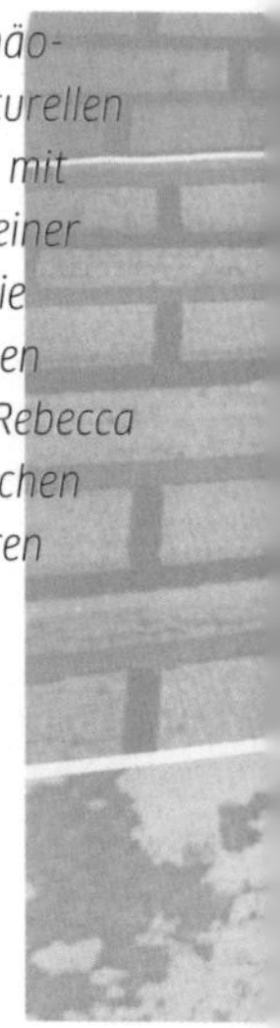

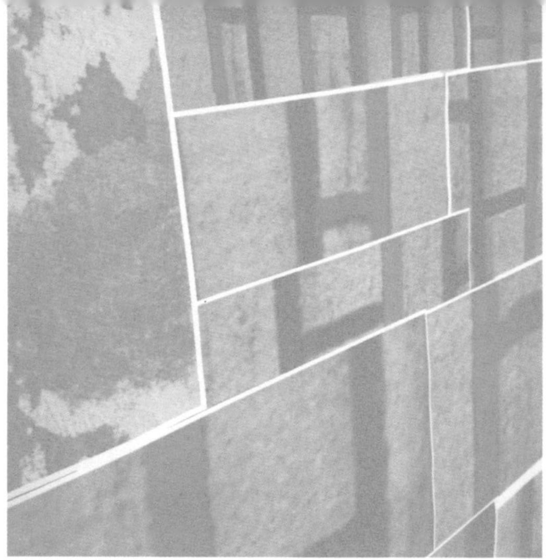

One day an artist from Germany was standing at the reception desk with a thick book under her arm: Christina Wildgrube. The book turned out to be a thesis that was written during Wildgrube's semester abroad at the University of Illinois at Chicago (UIC) with the wonderful title City and Typography in Search of Analogies. *For us, it was love at first sight – and Wildgrube became our first resident in the summer of 2017.*

Eines Tages stand eine Künstlerin aus Deutschland mit einem dicken Buch unter dem Arm an der Rezeption: Christina Wildgrube. Das Buch entpuppte sich als ihre Abschlussarbeit an der University of Illinois at Chicago (UIC), die während Wildgrubes Auslandssemesters dort entstanden war und den wunderbaren Titel City and Typography in Search of Analogies *trug. Für uns Liebe auf den ersten Blick – und Wildgrube wurde unsere erste Residentin im Sommer 2017.*

CHRISTINA WILDGRUBE RESIDENZ / SIEDLUNG TÖRTEN

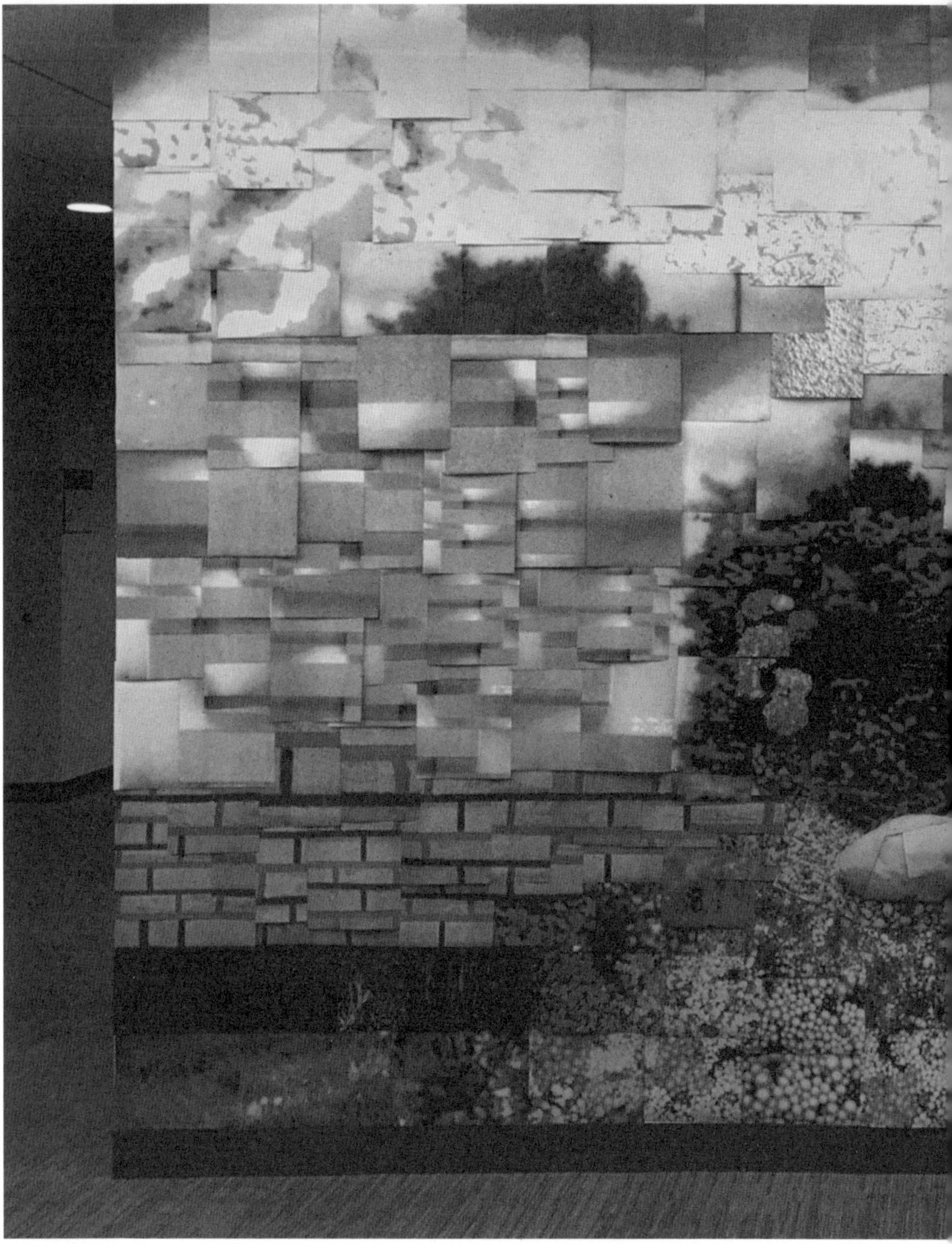

Many Gardens and Facades, 2017
Collage with photocopies of photographs of the 314 houses
Foyer Goethe-Institut Chicago, 98.4 × 157.5 inches

Many Gardens and Facades, 2017
Kopier-Collage aus Fotografien der 314 Häuser
Foyer Goethe-Institut Chicago, 98,4 × 157,5 Zoll

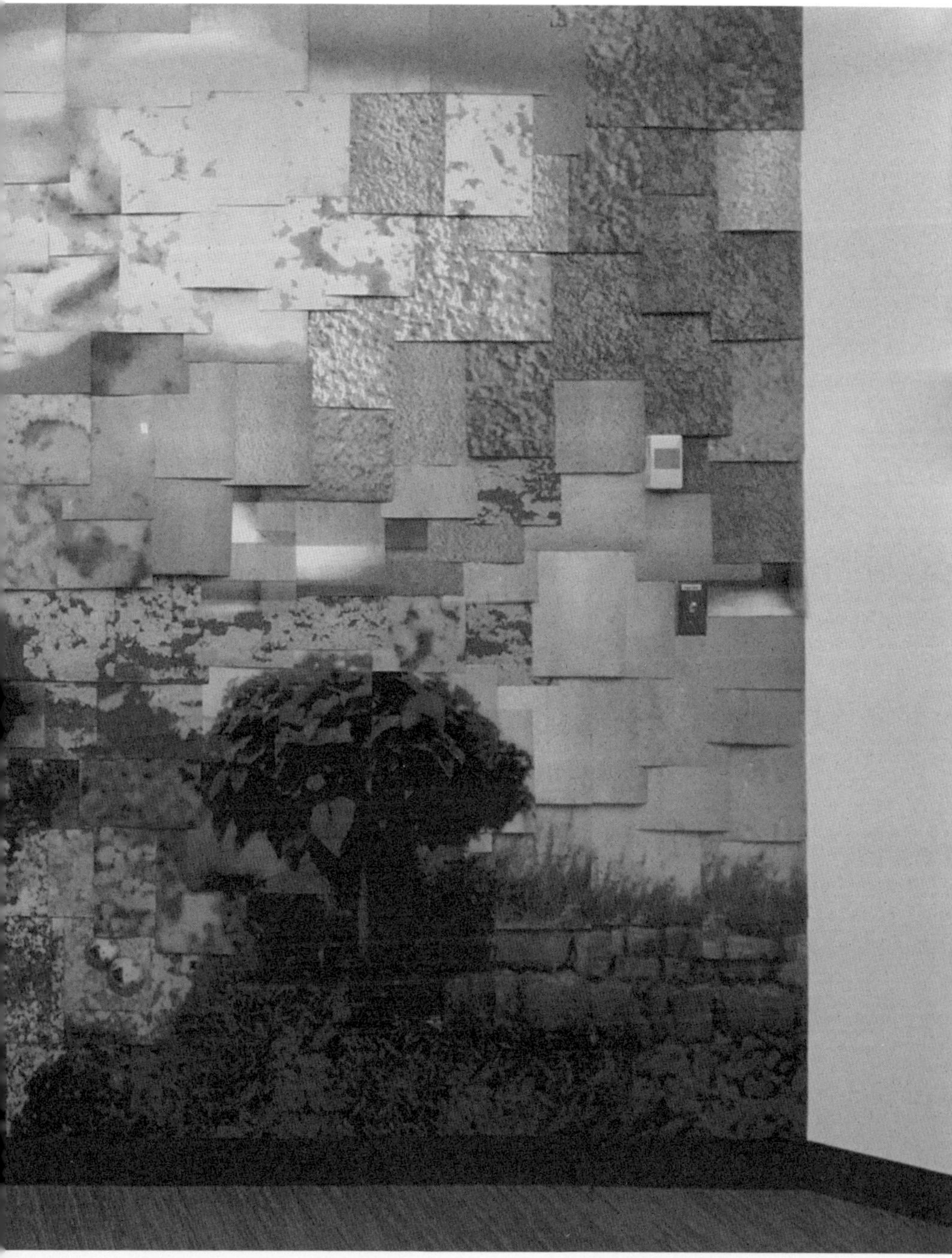

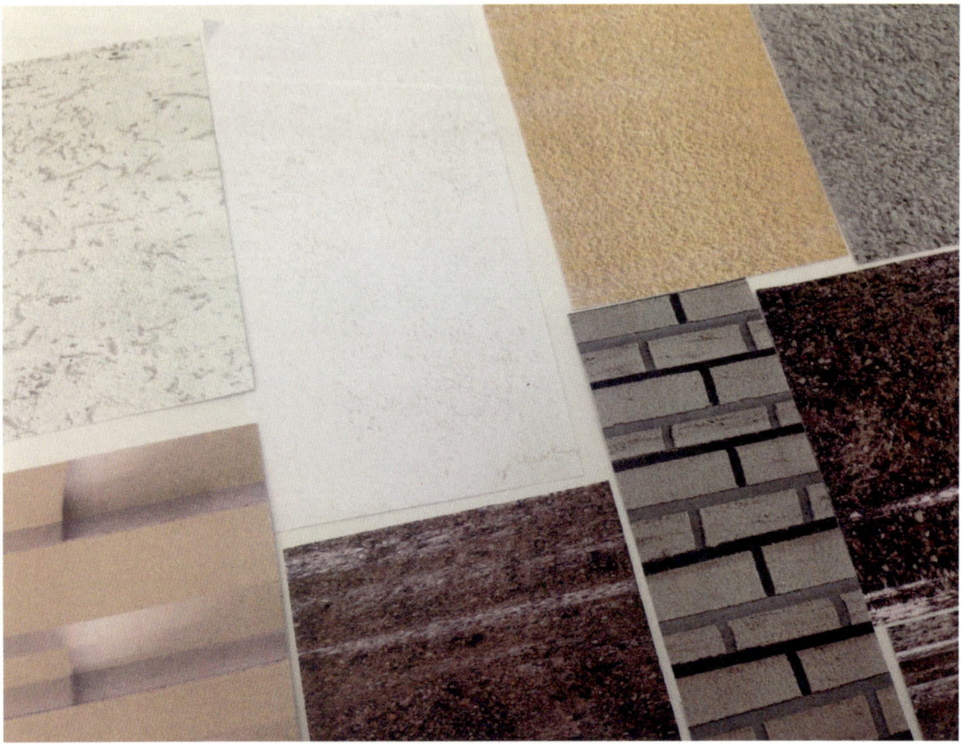

Scans of Facades, 2017 **Scans der Hausfassaden, 2017**

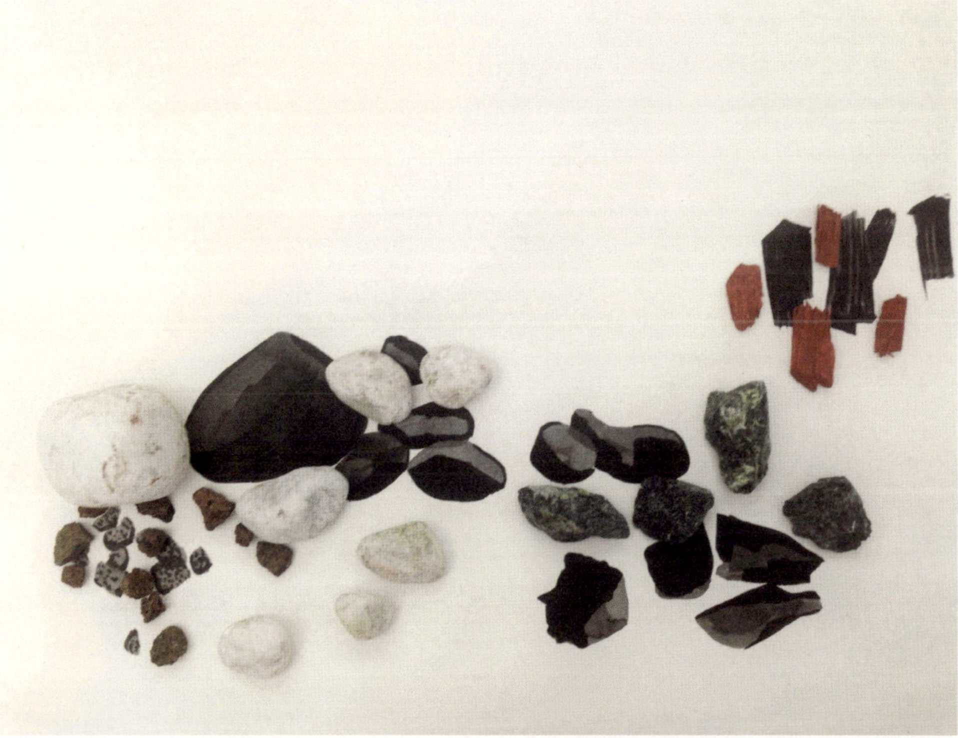

Collage of Materials, 2017
Stones, wood, ink-drawing

Materialcollage, 2017
Steine, Holz, Tuschezeichnung

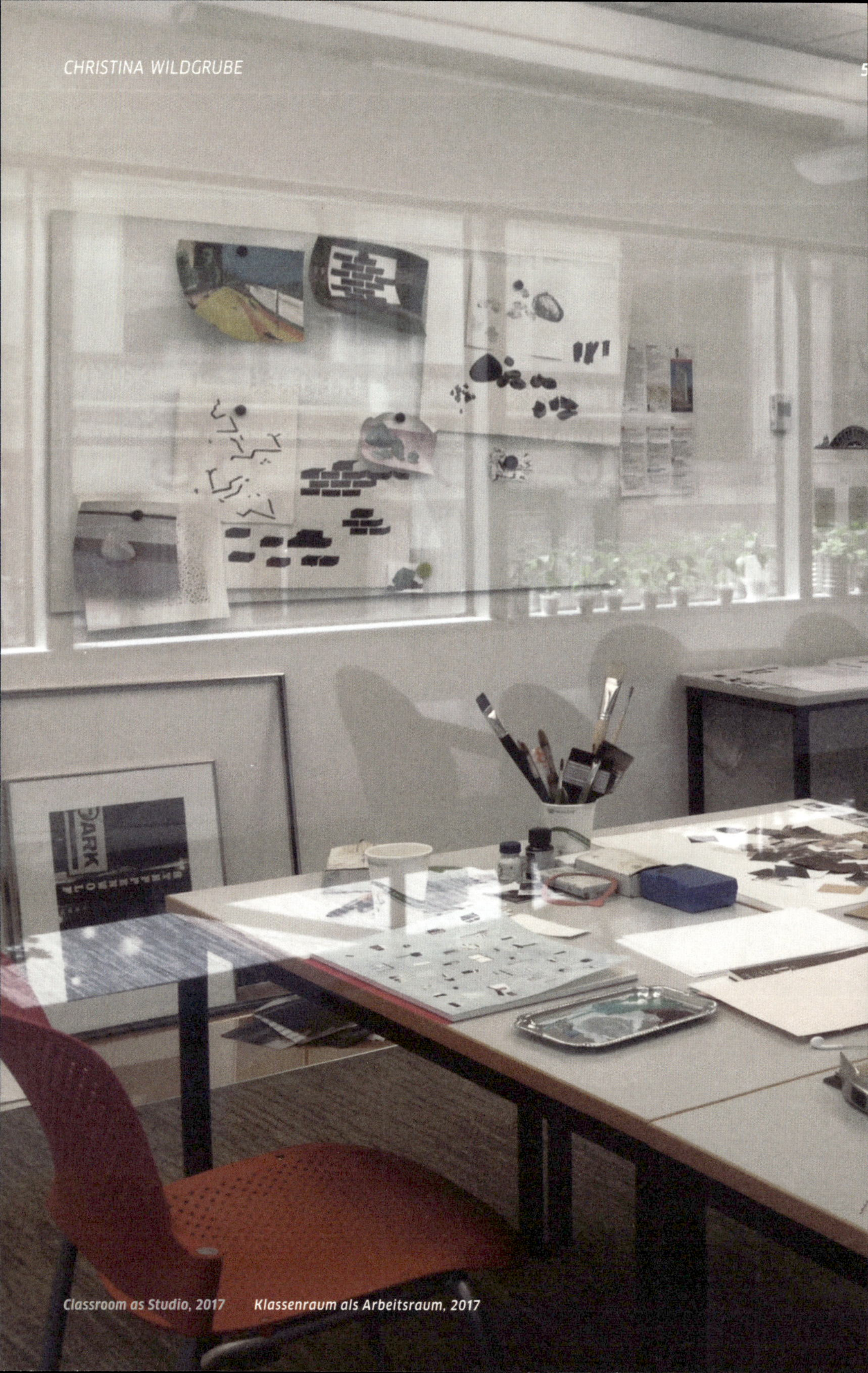

Classroom as Studio, 2017 *Klassenraum als Arbeitsraum, 2017*

1

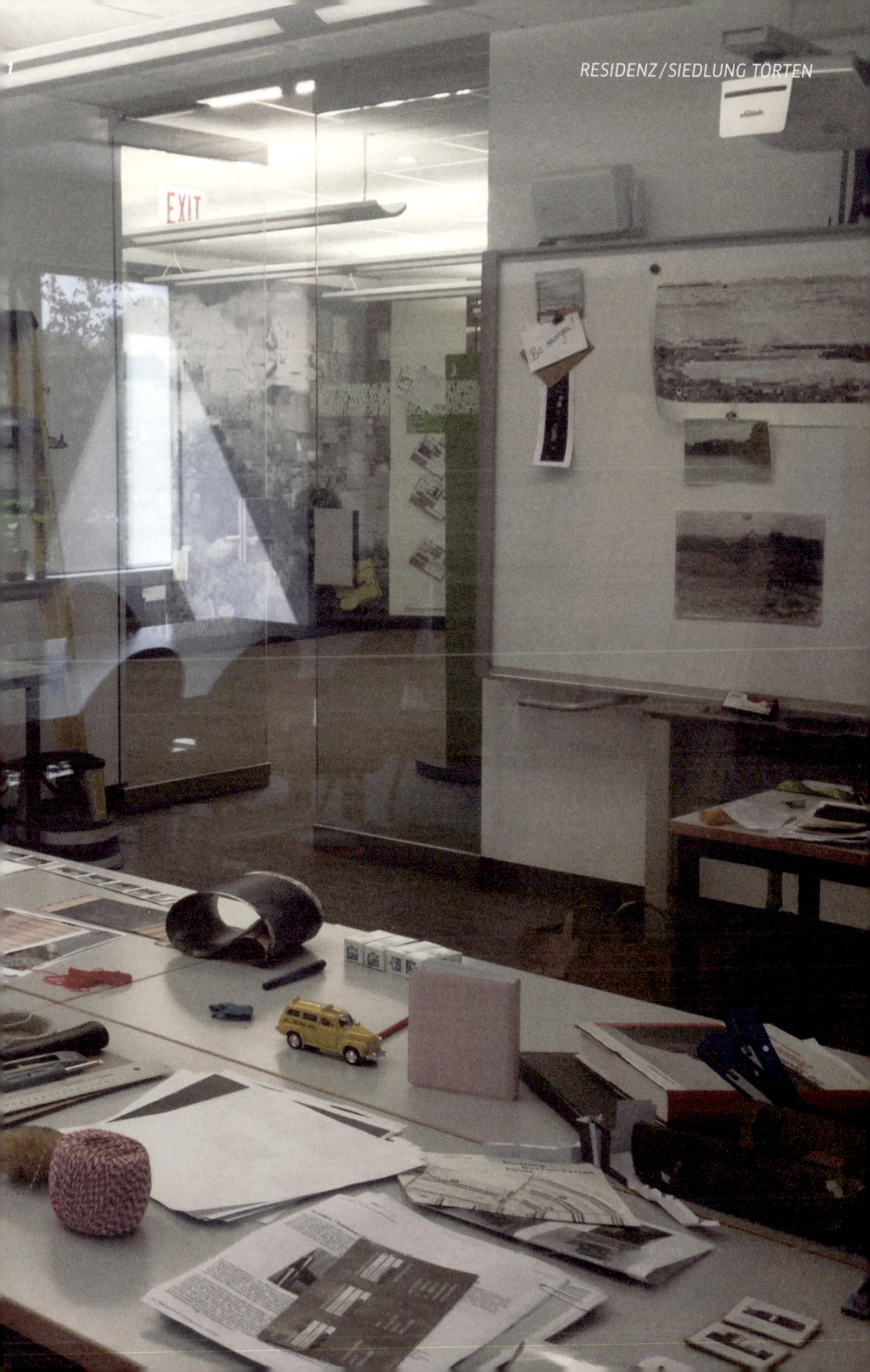

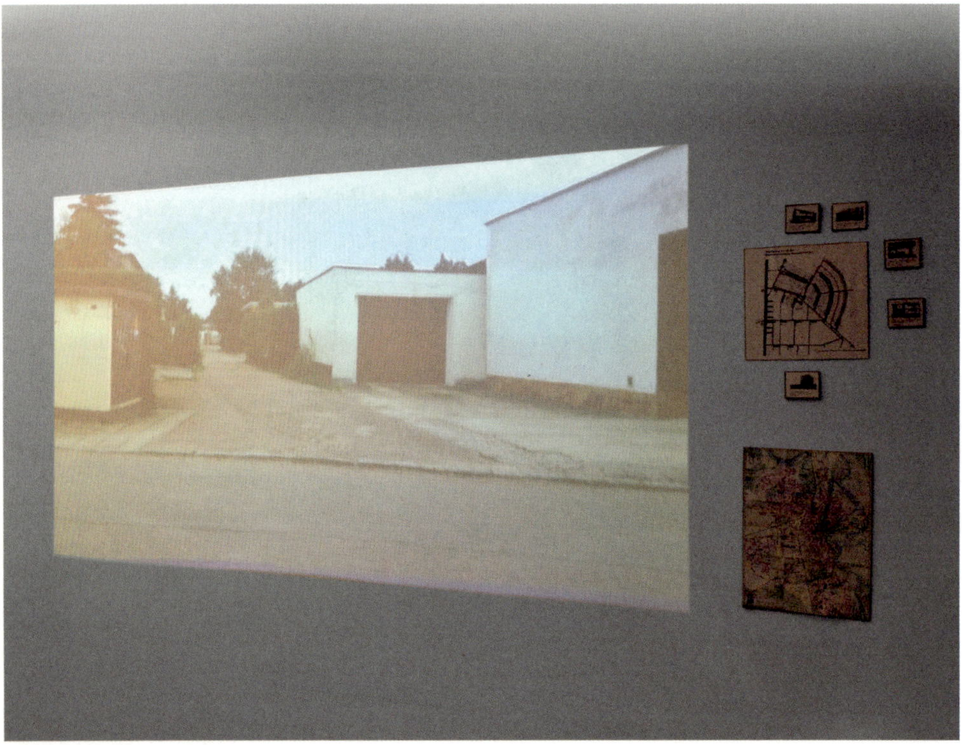

Road Trip Törten, 2017
Mobile-video, 11:11 min.

Road-Trip Törten, 2017
Handy-Video, 11:11 Min.

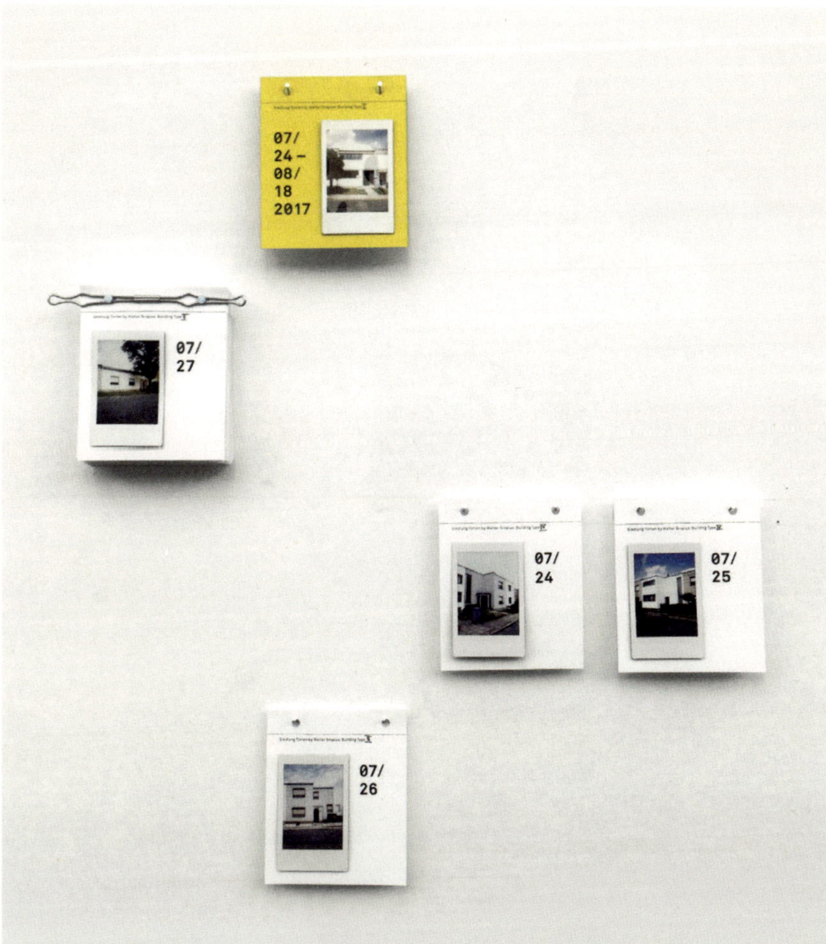

Everyday a new façade, 2017
Polaroid calender
07/14–08/18/2017

Everyday a new façade, 2017
Polaroid-Kalender
14/07–18/08/2017

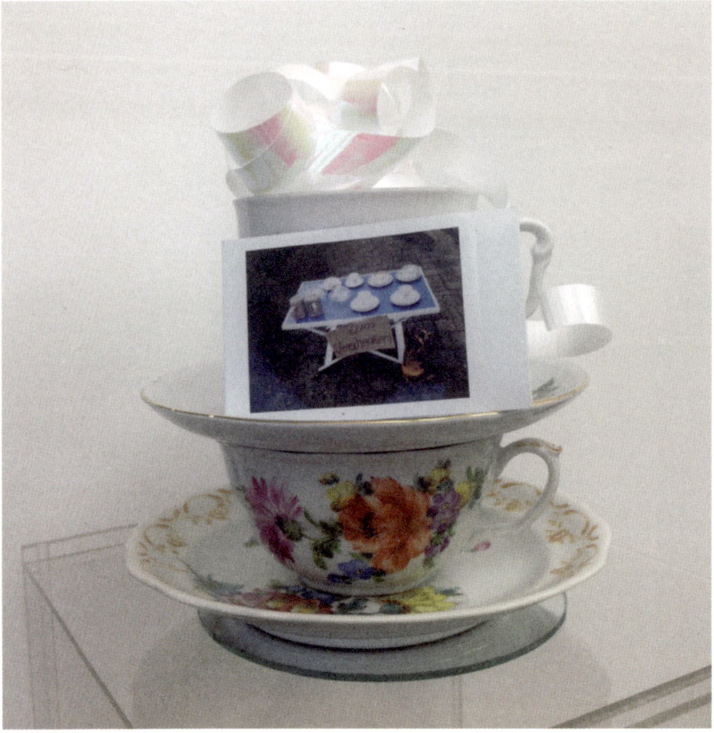

Törten-Tassen, 2017
Mirror, collector's cups, ribbon, polaroid photo
5.9 × 3.9 inches

Törten-Tassen, 2017
Spiegel, Sammeltassen, Schleifenband, Polaroidfoto
5.9 × 3,9 Zoll

314 × A GERMAN PLANNING URBAN HISTORY SIEDLUNG TÖRTEN

Christina Wildgrube

Siedlung Törten, a housing development of 314 houses with gardens for the city of Dessau, was designed by Walter Gropius and built between 1926 and 1928.

The single-family homes became the property of the inhabitants, who could modify the design as they saw fit. Consequently, the personal tastes and design sensibilities of the owners can be seen today.

In 1994, restrictions were put in place to prevent changes and remodeling projects within the estate. At first glance, the only recognizable common feature of the homes is their outline. Materials and exterior colors, windows, doors, and garden design deviate tremendously from the original plans: plastic doors from home improvement stores, boxwood hedges, stone-filled front yards, and heather. The difference between concept and reality attests to the further development of the estate. How it was altered from Gropius' plans to today's built environment is the topic of Christina Wildgrube's residency in Chicago.

During her residency at the Goethe-Institut, Wildgrube provided a visual inventory of the changes to the homes by means of photos and video material. She created the video work Road Trip Törten, *a Polaroid calendar named* Everyday a new façade, *and a photo collage visualizing the homes' essence entitled* Many Gardens and Façades.

314 × EINE DEUTSCHE STADTBAUGESCHICHTE SIEDLUNG TÖRTEN

Christina Wildgrube

Die von Walter Gropius entworfene Siedlung Dessau-Törten, eine im Auftrag der Stadt errichtete Reihenhaussiedlung mit Nutzgärten, entstand in den Jahren 1926 bis 1928. Die Einfamilienhäuser gingen dann in das Eigentum der Bewohner über, welche die Gestaltung nach Belieben verändern konnten.

So sind der persönliche Geschmack und das individuelle gestalterische Empfinden der Besitzer bis heute ablesbar. 1994 wurden Auflagen eingeführt, um Änderungs- und Umbaumaßnahmen in der Siedlung einen Riegel vorzuschieben. Die einzige Gemeinsamkeit der Bauten findet sich auf den ersten Blick in den Haussilhouetten. Die Materialien und die im Außenbereich verwendeten Farben, Fenster, Türen und Gartenanlagen weichen erheblich von der ursprünglichen Planung ab: Kunststofftüren vom Baumarkt, Buchsbaumhecken, Steingärten und Heidekraut.

Die Entwicklung der Siedlung verdeutlicht die Kluft zwischen Idee und Realität. Christina Wildgrube beschäftigt sich im Rahmen ihrer Residenz in Chicago mit dem veränderten Erscheinungsbild der heutigen Anlage gegenüber dem Planungskonzept von Gropius.

Während ihrer Residenz am Goethe-Institut erstellte Wildgrube anhand von Fotografien und Videomaterial ein visuelles Inventar der Veränderungen, die an den Bauten vorgenommen wurden. Sie erstellte das Video Road-Trip Törten, *den Polaroid-Kalender* Everyday a new façade *und eine Fotocollage zum Wesen und der Essenz der Häuser unter dem Titel* Many Gardens and Façades.

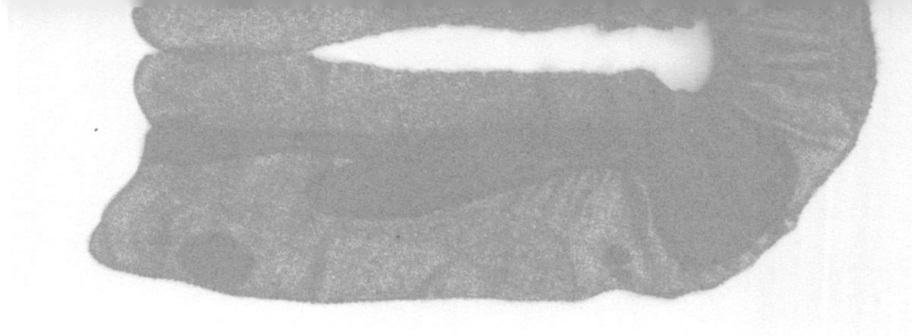

Anke Loh studied at the Royal Academy of Fine Arts Antwerp and designed costumes for Rosas / Anne Teresa de Keersmaeker and for Kobalt Works / Arco Renz. The native East Westphalian has lived in Chicago since 2005. In order to try out material, she works with knitting experts and with the help of knitting machines in Tilburg. The Goethe-Institut Chicago is offering Loh a place to try out smaller installations before exhibitions.

*Anke Loh studierte an der Koninklijke Academie voor Schone Kunsten Antwerpen und entwarf danach Kostüme für die Kompanie Rosas und Arco Renz in Belgien. Die gebürtige Ostwestfälin lebt seit 2005 in Chicago. Um Material auszuprobieren, arbeitet sie mit Strickexpert*innen und unter Zuhilfenahme von Strickmaschinen in Tilburg. Das Goethe-Institut Chicago bietet Loh einen Ort, um vor Ausstellungen kleinere Installationen auszuprobieren.*

ANKE LOH
INTERKNIT

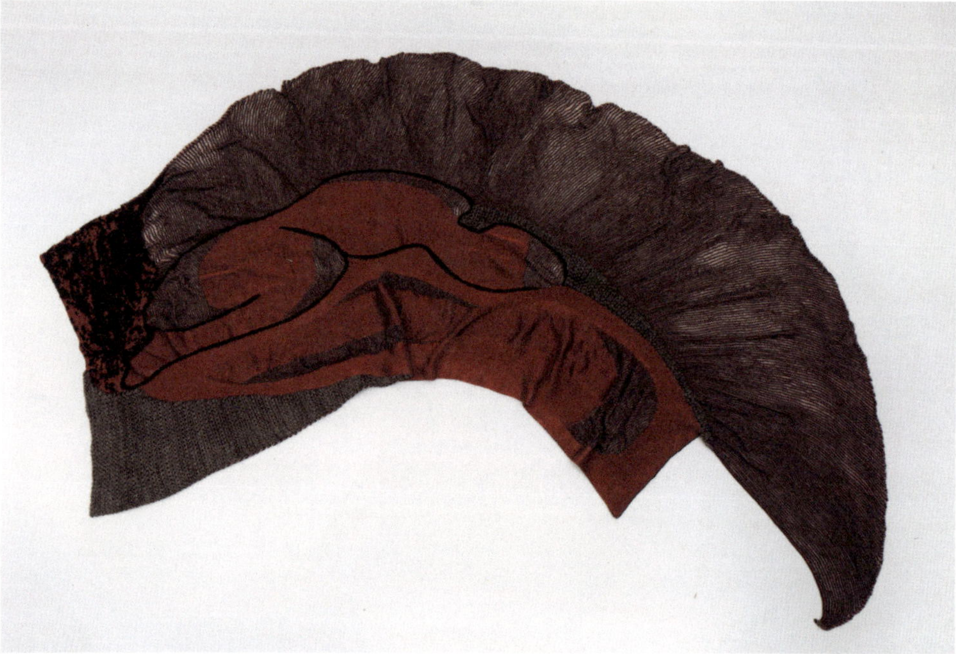

Interknit, Figure 4, 2018
Long throw, mixed yarns, red/brown
33 × 86 inches

Interknit, Figure 4, 2018
Großer Überwurf, Mischgarn, rot/braun
33 × 86 Zoll

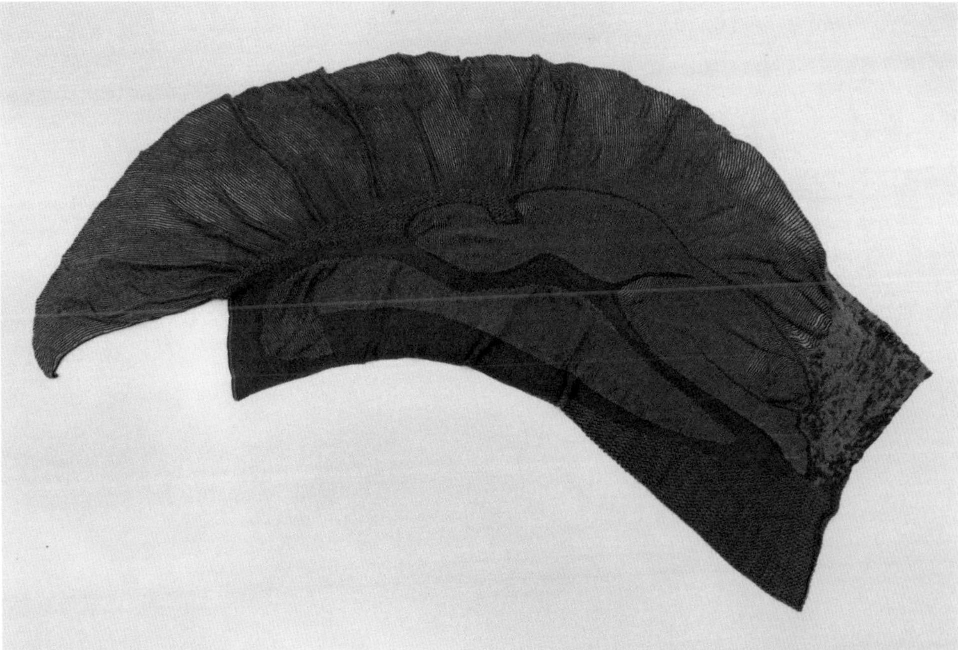

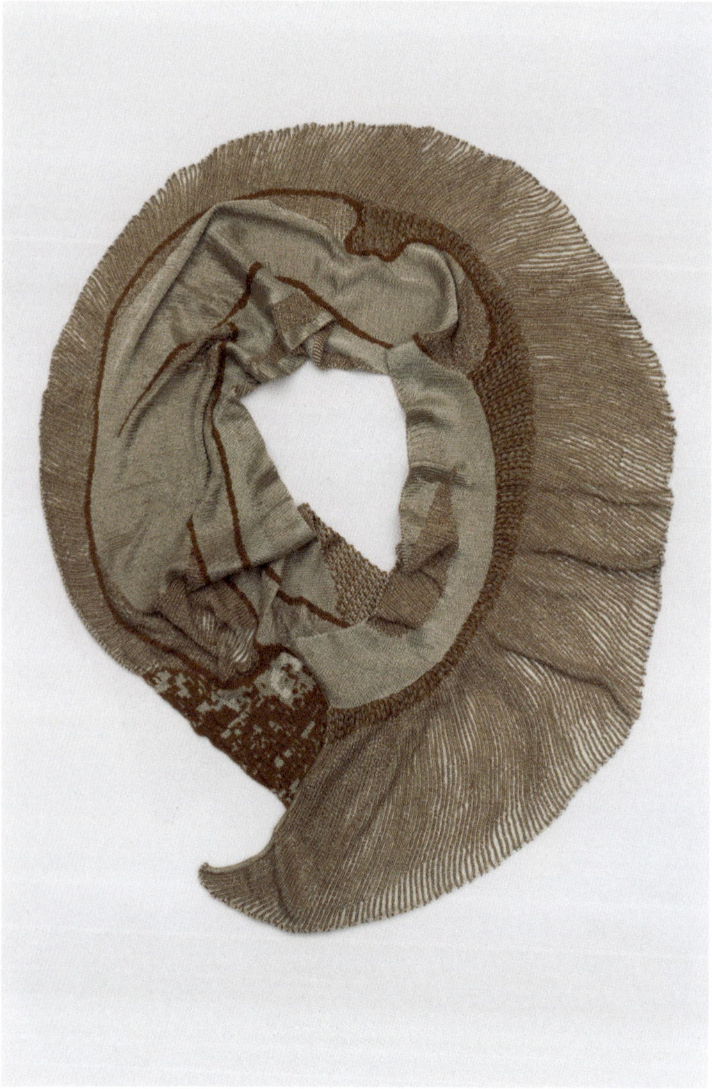

Interknit, Figure 4, 2018
Large scarf, mixed yarns, cream/gold
15 × 82 inches

Interknit, Figure 4, 2018
Großer Schal, Mischgarn, cremefarben/gold
15 × 82 Zoll

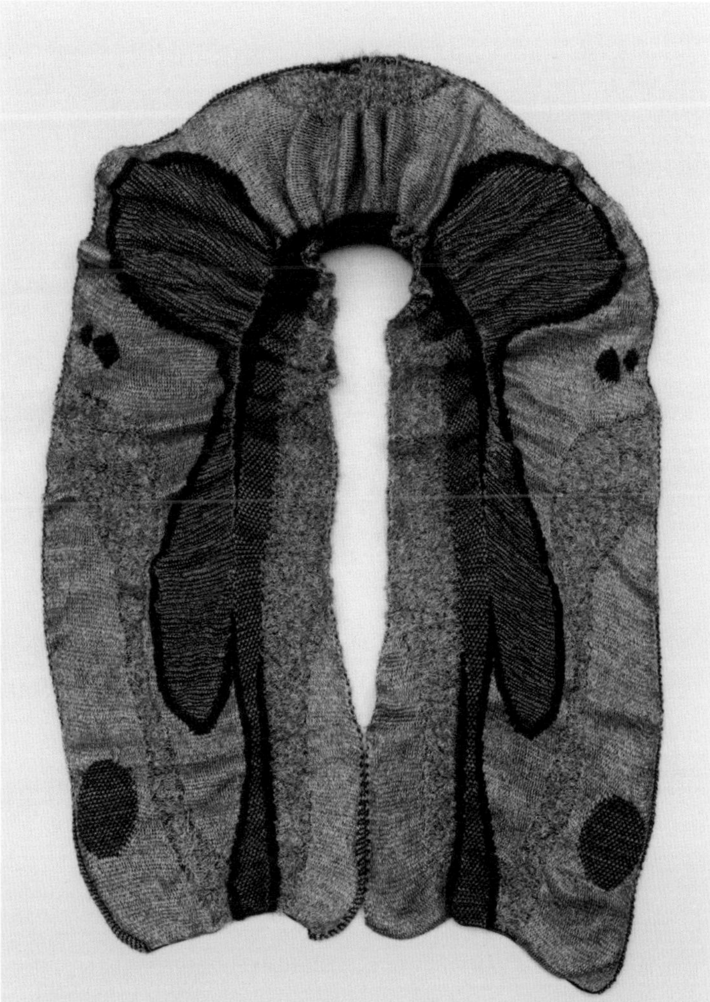

Interknit, no title, 2018
Long throw, mixed yarns, metallic, green/navy
15 × 116 inches

Interknit, no title, 2018
Großer Überwurf, Mischgarn, metallisch, grün/marineblau
15 × 116 Zoll

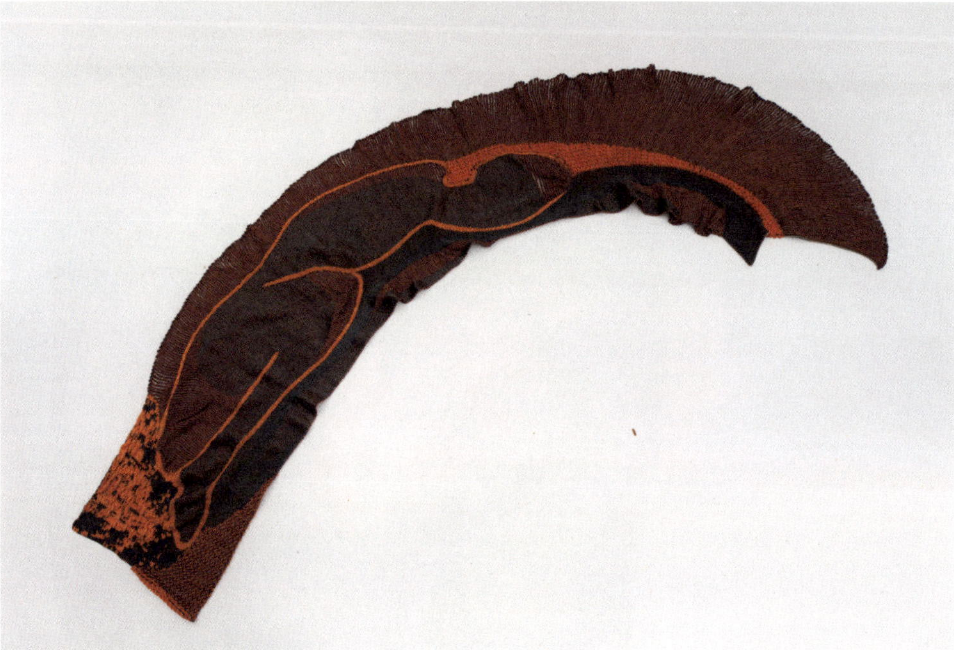

Interknit, Figure 4, 2018
Large scarf, mixed yarns, orange/grey
15 × 82 inches

Interknit, Figure 4, 2018
Großer Schal, Mischgarn, orange/grau
15 × 82 Zoll

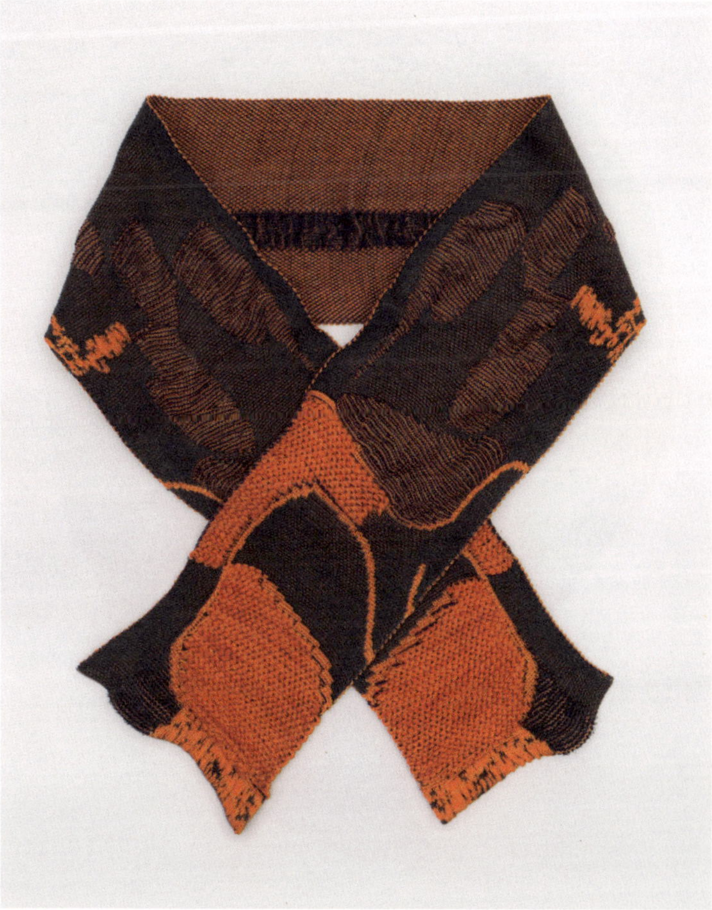

Interknit, no title, 2018
Small scarf, mixed yarns, orange/grey
7 × 65 inches

Interknit, no title, 2018
Kleiner Schal, Mischgarn, orange/grau
7 × 65 Zoll

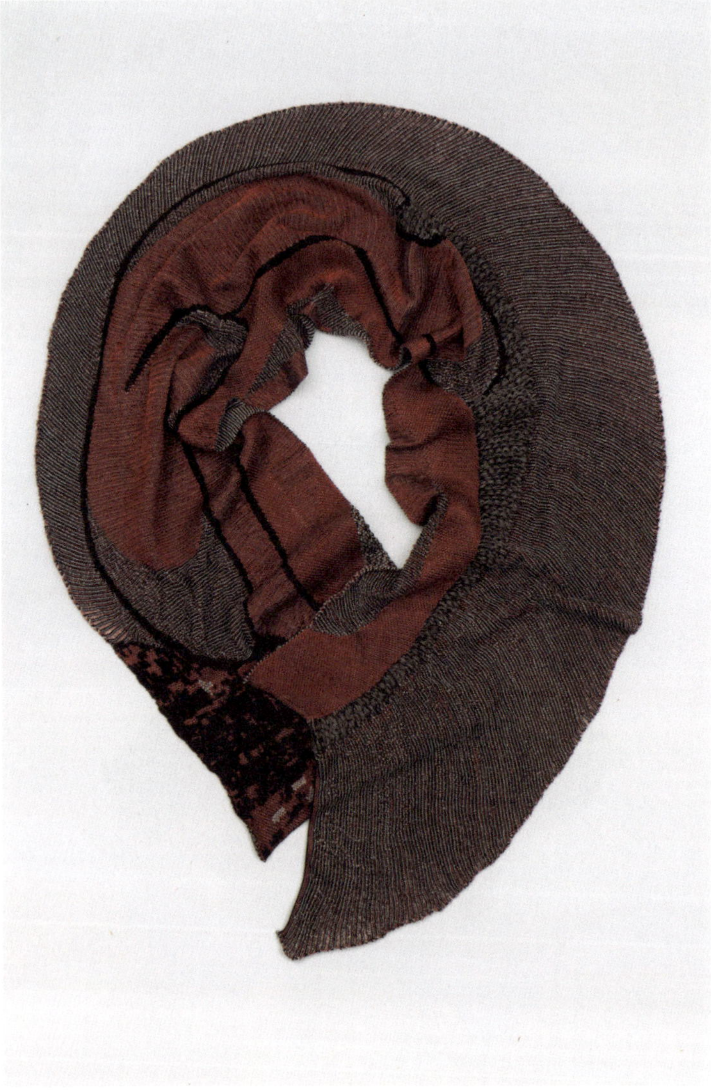

Interknit, Figure 4, 2018
Large Scarf, mixed yarns, red/brown
15 × 82 inches

Interknit, Figure 4, 2018
Großer Schal, Mischgarn, rot/braun
15 × 82 Zoll

INTERKNIT

Anke Loh

Loh embraces technology as another way of communicating with the body – extending the body to communicate with the outside world as well as the inner world of one's self. She has forged multiple collaborations with technology-focused individuals, research teams, companies and universities in Europe, Asia and the USA, with the objective of blending fashion with the latest technological advances. She focuses on discovering new ways to incorporate fiber optics into fabric. Currently, she is blending refined craftwork with high-tech resources, as she develops new directions with her latest work, employing state-of-the-art Stoll knitting machines during her residencies at TextielLab in Tilburg, the Netherlands.

Anke Loh's collection of knits revolves around women's stories – their opportunities, challenges, delights, and anxieties. Each piece combines bold yet delicate textures and patterns, evoking women who break free from expectation and tradition. The color combinations and select yarns mix lengths, weights, textures, synthetic, and natural fibers, intended to enhance the infinite possibilities of the female form.

INTERKNIT

Anke Loh

Anke Loh versteht Technologie als alternatives Kommunikationsmedium für den Körper – als Erweiterung des Körpers, um sowohl mit der äußeren als auch der inneren Welt zu kommunizieren. Sie initiierte verschiedene Gemeinschaftsprojekte mit technologieorientierten Partnern, Forschungsgruppen, Unternehmen und Universitäten in Europa, Asien und den USA, um Mode und den neuesten technologischen Fortschritt zusammenzubringen. Sie beschäftigt sich in erster Linie mit der Integration von Faseroptik in Textilien. In ihren neuesten Arbeiten erforscht sie innovative Richtungen und verknüpft hohe Handwerkskunst mit High-Tech-Ressourcen. Im Rahmen ihrer Residenzen bei TextielLab im niederländischen Tilburg setzt sie modernste Strickmaschinen von Stoll ein.

Anke Lohs Strickkollektion erzählt Geschichten von Frauen – ihre Chancen, Herausforderungen, Freuden und Ängste. Jedes Stück verwebt kühne und gleichzeitig filigrane Strukturen und Muster und erinnert an Frauen, die aus Erwartungshaltungen und Traditionen ausbrechen. Bei den Farbzusammenstellungen und ausgewählten Garnen werden Längen, Gewichte, Beschaffenheiten, künstliche und natürliche Fasern kombiniert. Sie stehen für die endlosen Möglichkeiten, die dem Weiblichen eigen sind.

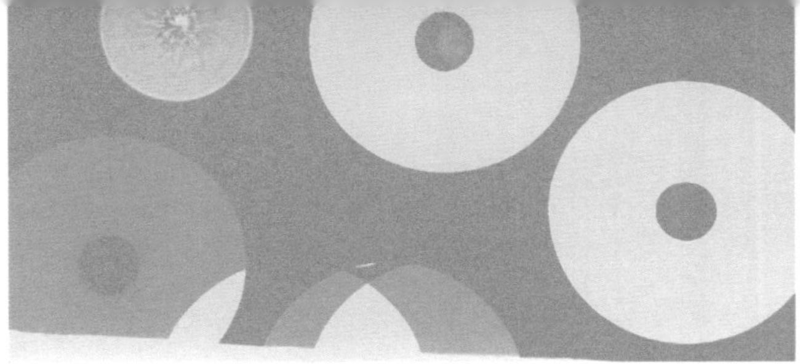

Almost every institution in Chicago presenting photography exhibitions includes Doug Fogelson's work. In addition to his work as an artist, he is active in the grassroots movement, which offers many young people their first contact with art. Moreover, together with Openlands he developed a project entitled O. L. A. F. T.: Open Art Land and Fact Team.

Es gibt in Chicago kaum eine Institution, die Fotoausstellungen präsentiert, in der Doug Fogelsons Arbeiten nicht vertreten sind. Neben seiner Arbeit als Künstler ist er aktiv in der Graswurzelbewegung, die vielen jungen Menschen den ersten Kontakt mit Kunst ermöglicht, und mit Openlands entwickelte er gemeinsam ein Projekt mit dem Titel O. L. A. F. T.: Open Art Land and Fact Team.

DOUG FOGELSON
FORMS & RECORDS

Forms & Records BW, 2014–2015
Photogram, silver gelatin print, 20 × 16 inches
Pp. 68–74

Forms & Records BW, 2014–2015
Fotogramm, Silbergelatine-Abzug, 20 × 16 Zoll
S. 68–74

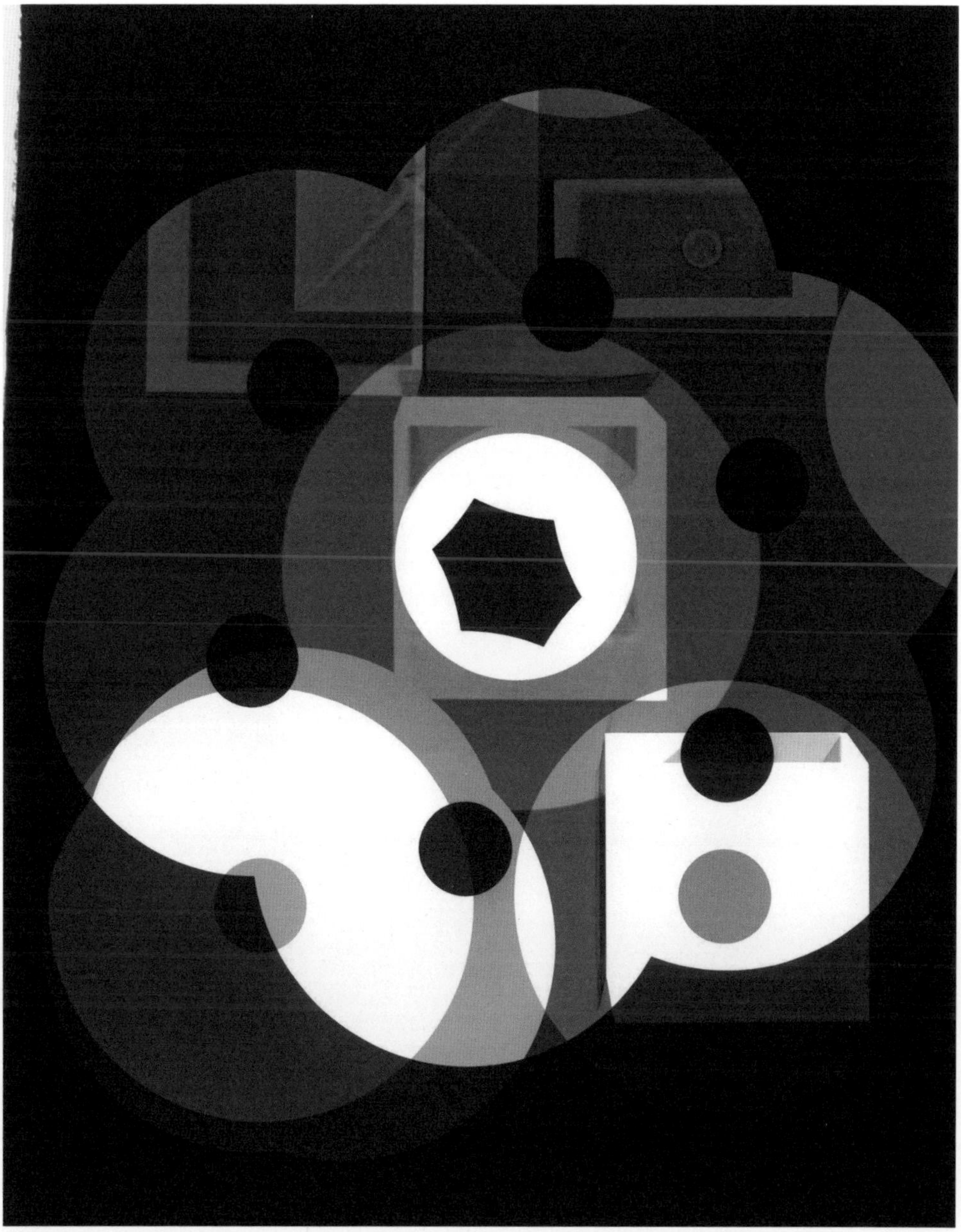

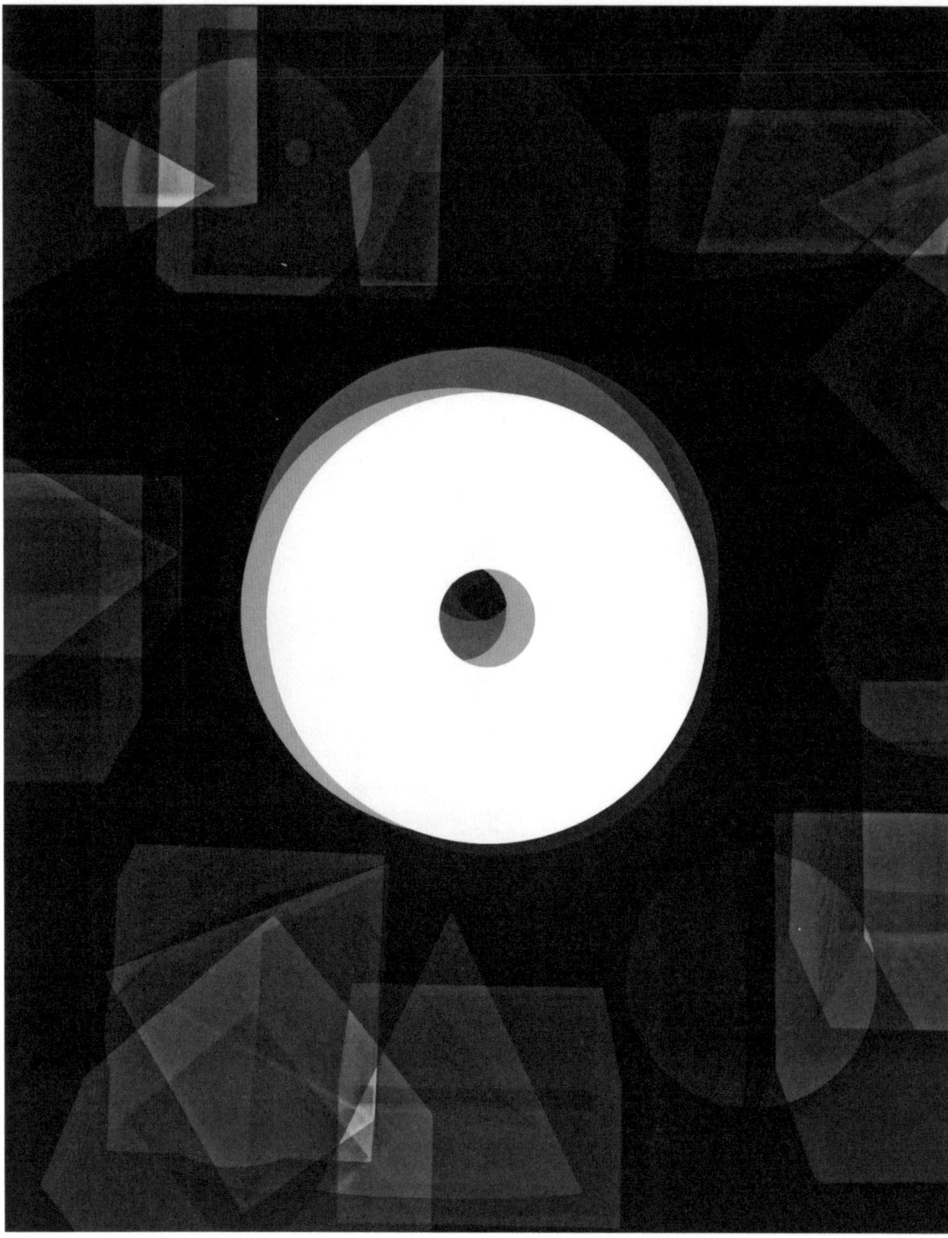

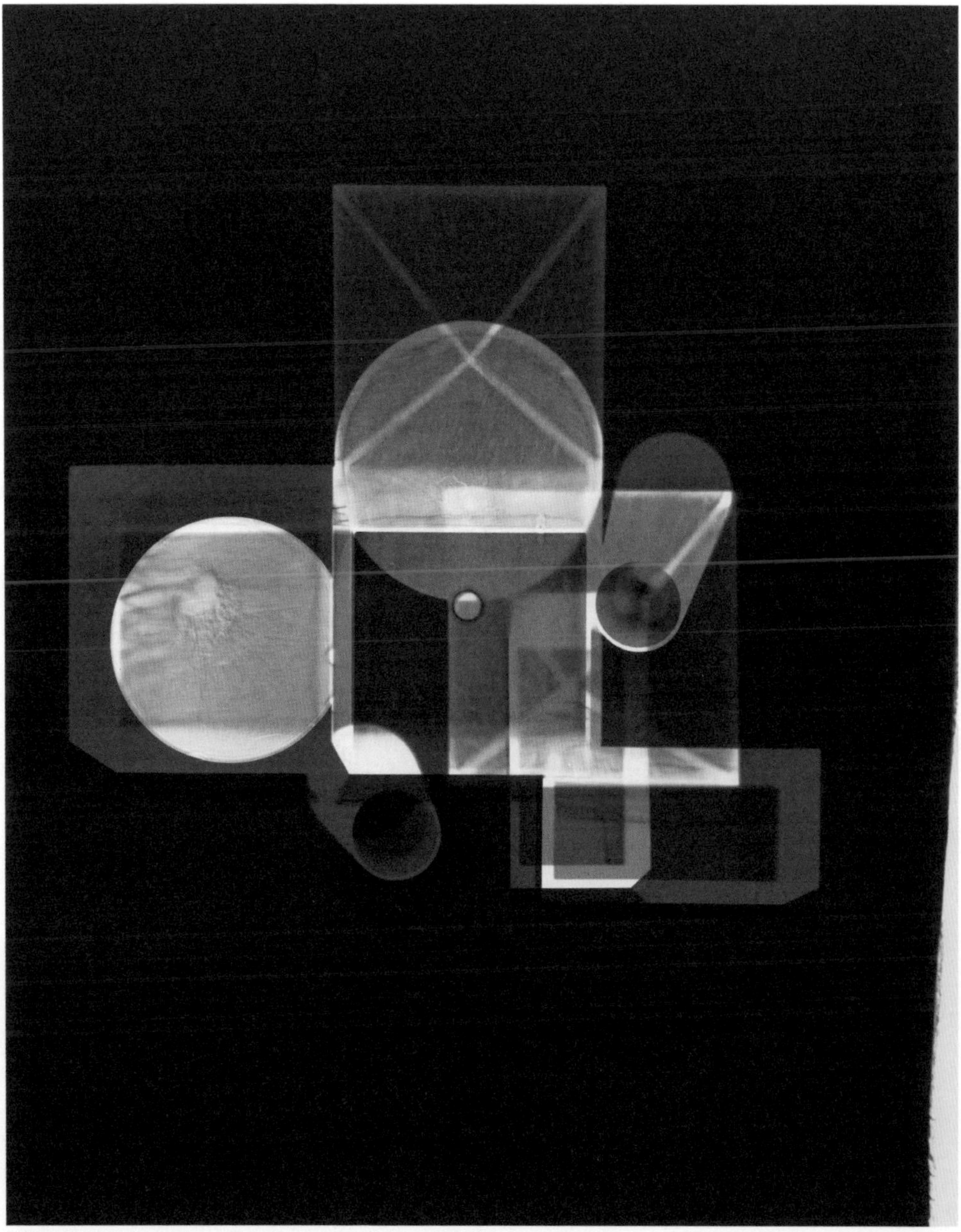

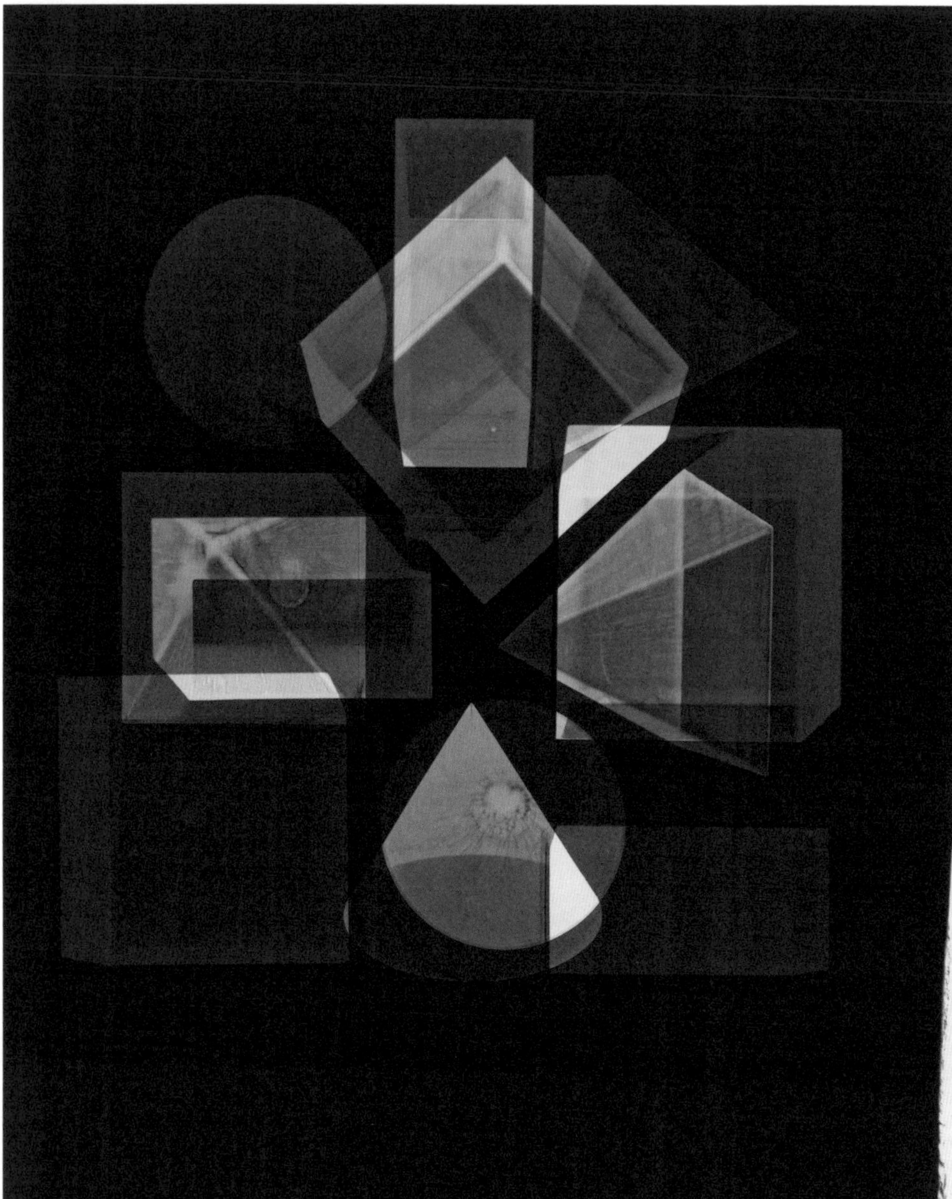

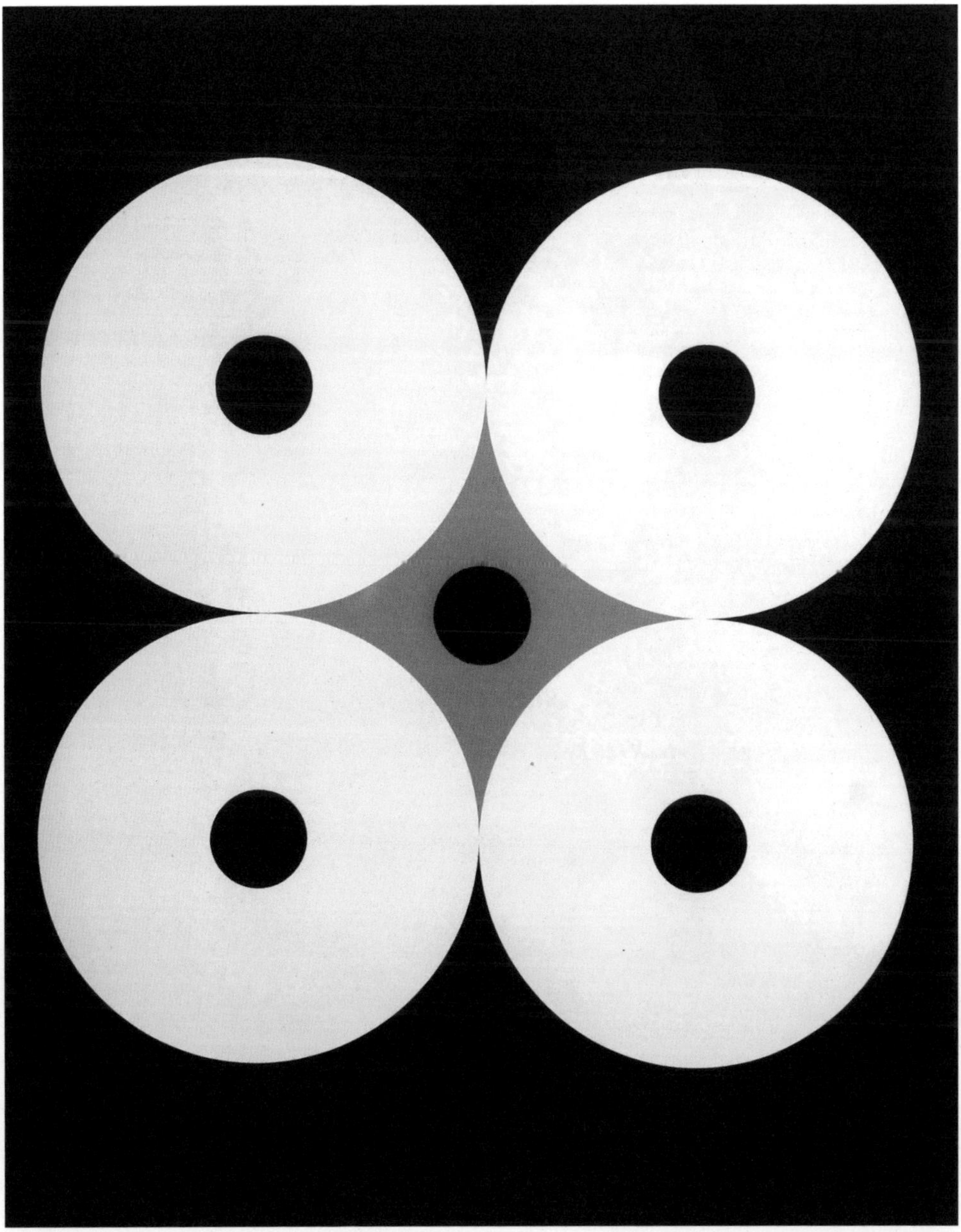

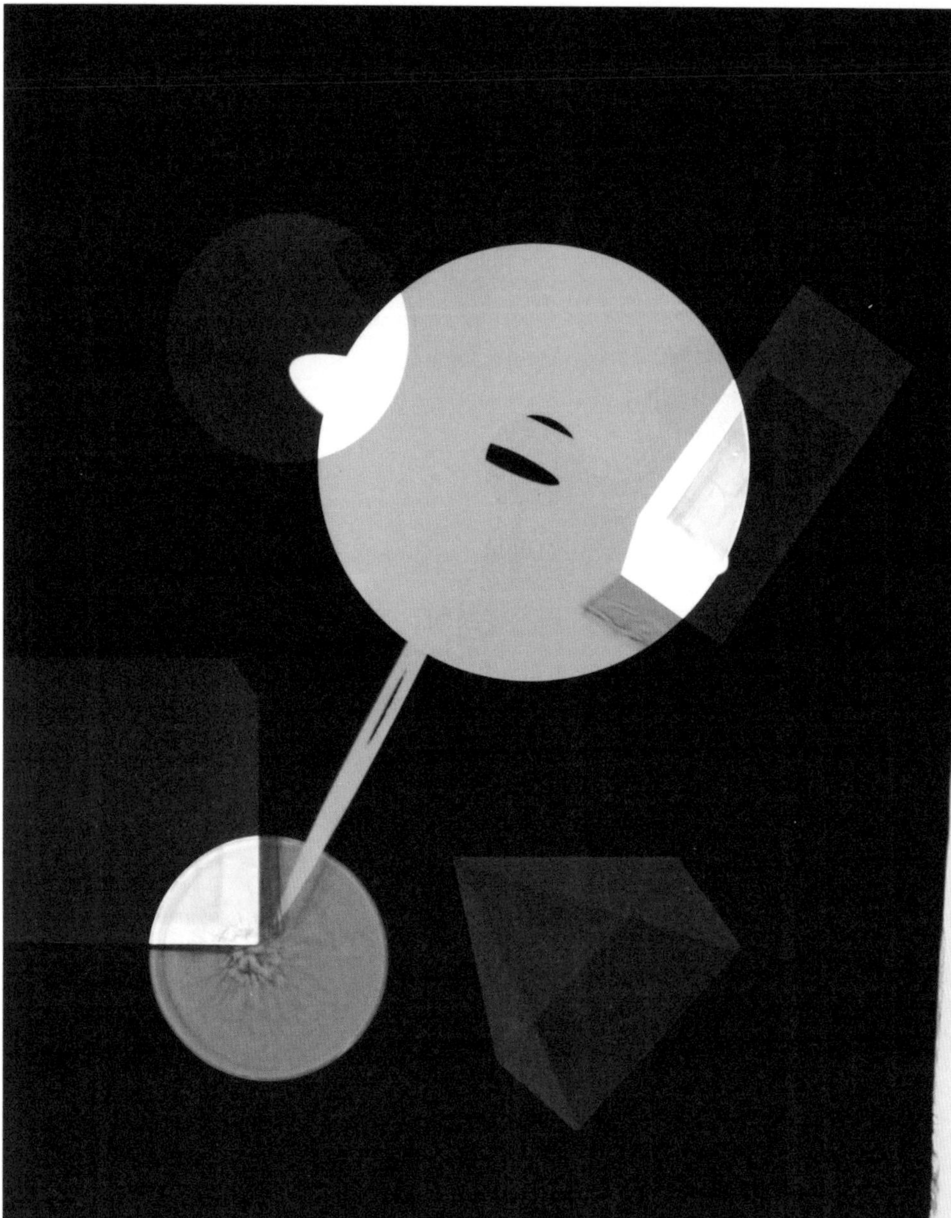

FORMS & RECORDS

Doug Fogelson

I produced photograms by exposing geometric and scale-model architectural forms together with vintage 7" inch audio records (aka 45's). Some of the forms used were collected via student projects a the IIT Institute of Design and the records chosen from specific artists of the late 1950's and 1960's. I used simple three dimensional plastic geometric forms to riff on the investigation of, "Color-Form Correspondence" by Kandinsky at the original Bauhaus in the 1920's. As shadow-record photograms are brief, latent moments where materials interacted, they can also articulate a new typology as created by the flattening of such selected materials. My photograms were the final project to be made in the original darkroom of the New Bauhaus at that time, which was located in the basement of Mies Van der Rohe's Crown Hall at the Institute of Design/IIT campus, before the area got remodeled.

FORMS & RECORDS

Doug Fogelson

*Ich habe Fotogramme erstellt, indem ich maßstabsgetreue Architekturmodelle zusammen mit traditionellen 7-Zoll-Schallplatten (sog. 45er) belichtete. Die Modelle stammten von Student*innen und die Schallplatten von ausgewählten Künstler*innen der späten 1950er und 1960er Jahre. Da Fotogramme mit ihrem Schattenspiel flüchtige Augenblicke festhalten, in denen Materialien miteinander interagieren, können sie in Abhängigkeit von den gewählten Elementen auch eine neue Typologie artikulieren. Meine Farb- und Schwarz- /Weiß-Aufnahmen sind die letzten Arbeiten, die in der Originaldunkelkammer des New Bauhaus entstanden, die im Untergeschoss der von Mies van der Rohe entworfenen Crown Hall am Institute of Design/IIT Campus untergebracht war, bevor der Bereich umgebaut wurde.*

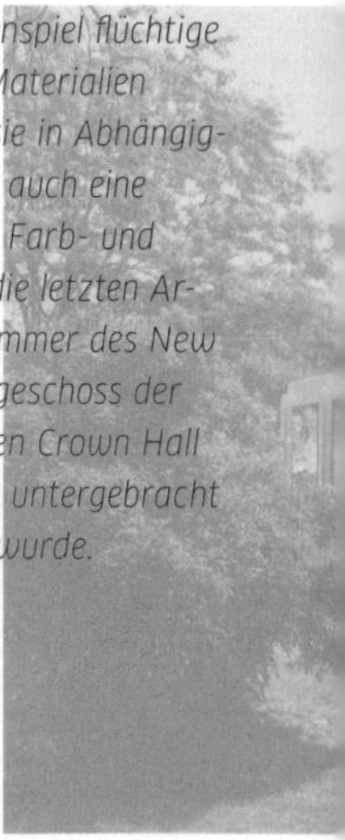

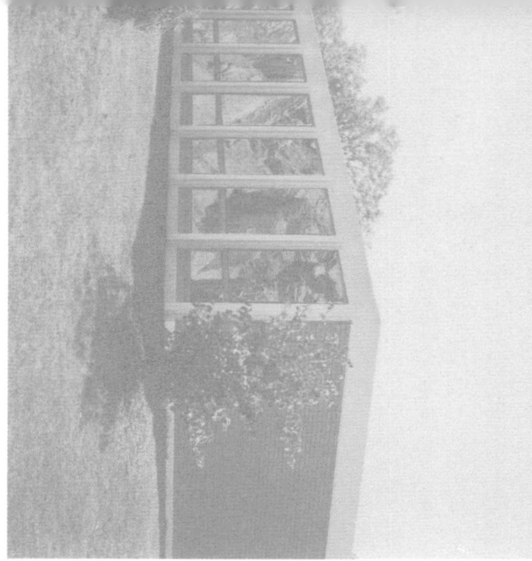

When we met, we immediately had a specific idea for an exhibition at the Goethe-Institut: Assaf Evron's show entitled Basel Street 54. Trait pour trait, *a scene rebuilt in colorful tiles bearing the ornamentation and decorations of the buildings on Tel Aviv's Basel Street in the Bauhaus style. Beautiful! Unfortunately, we have not yet been able to realize this idea. But we helped bring a very different idea into the world, namely projecting collages in the windows of Mies' buildings.*

Als wir uns kennenlernten, hatten wir sofort eine klare Idee für eine Ausstellung am Goethe-Institut: Evrons Ausstellung mit dem Titel Basel Street 54, Trait pour trait, *eine aus bunten Kacheln nachgebaute Szenerie der Ornamentik und Dekorationen der Häuser in der Basel Street in Tel Aviv im Bauhausstil. Wunderschön! Wir konnten sie leider bis heute nicht umsetzen. Aber wir halfen einer ganz anderen Idee in die Welt: Collagen in die Fenster von Mies' Wohnhäusern zu projizieren.*

ASSAF EVRON
COLLAGES

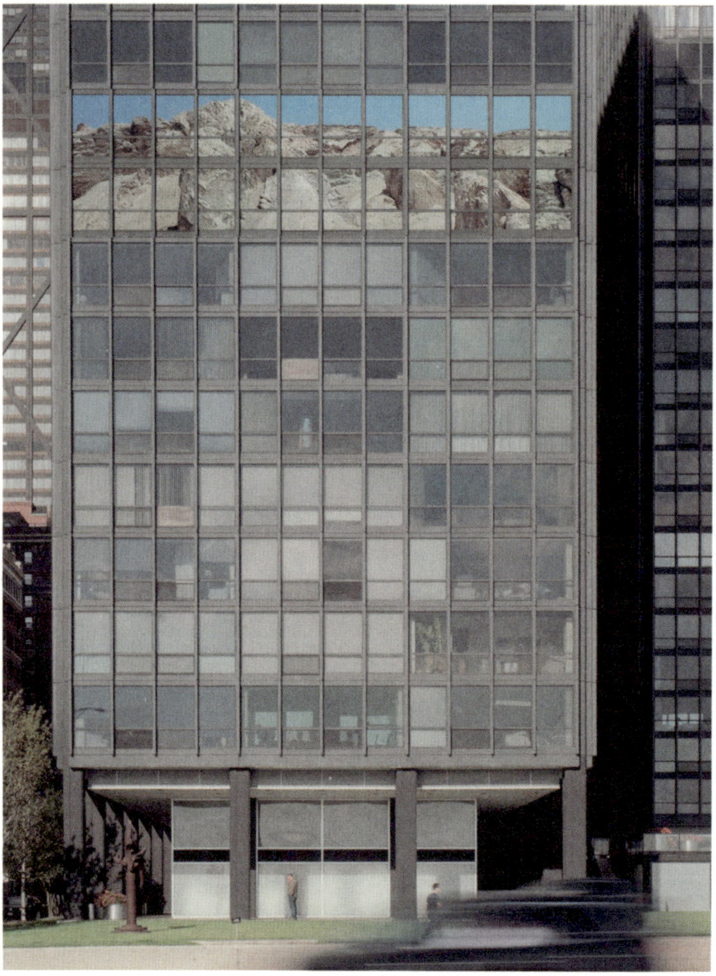

Concept Collage for 900–910 Lake Shore Drive, 2017–2018
Pigment print, collage
25 × 20 inches

Concept Collage for 900–910 Lake Shore Drive, 2017–2018
Pigmentdruck, Collage
25 × 20 Zoll

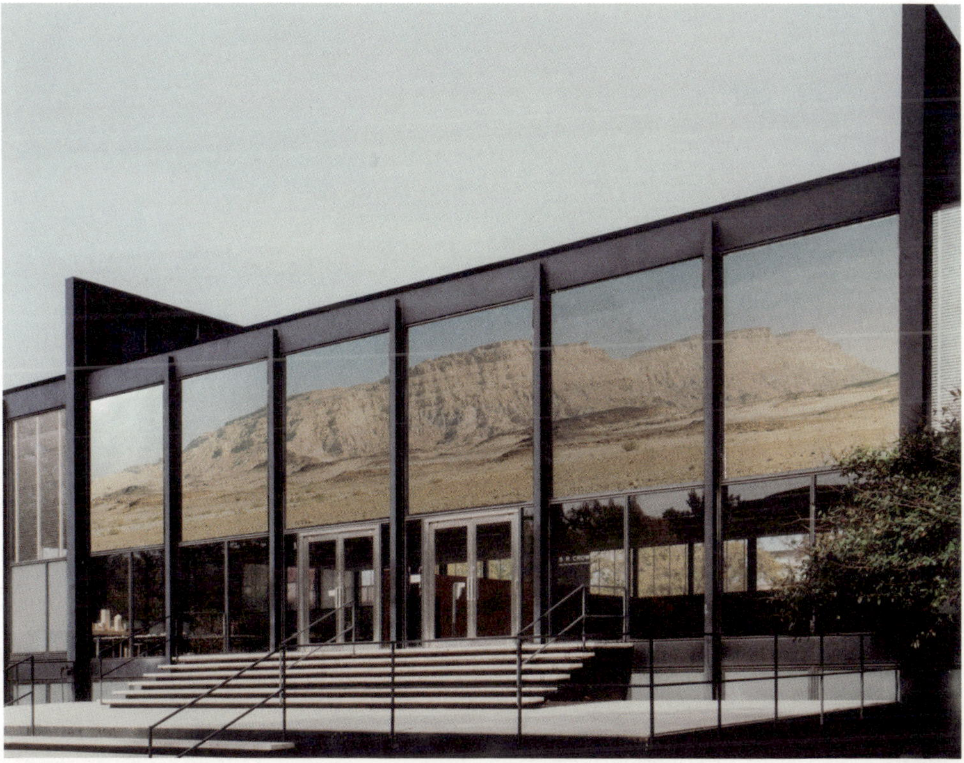

Concept Collage for S. R. Crown Hall, 2017–2018
Pigment print, collage
16 × 20 inches

Concept Collage for S. R. Crown Hall, 2017–2018
Pigmentdruck, collage
16 × 20 Zoll

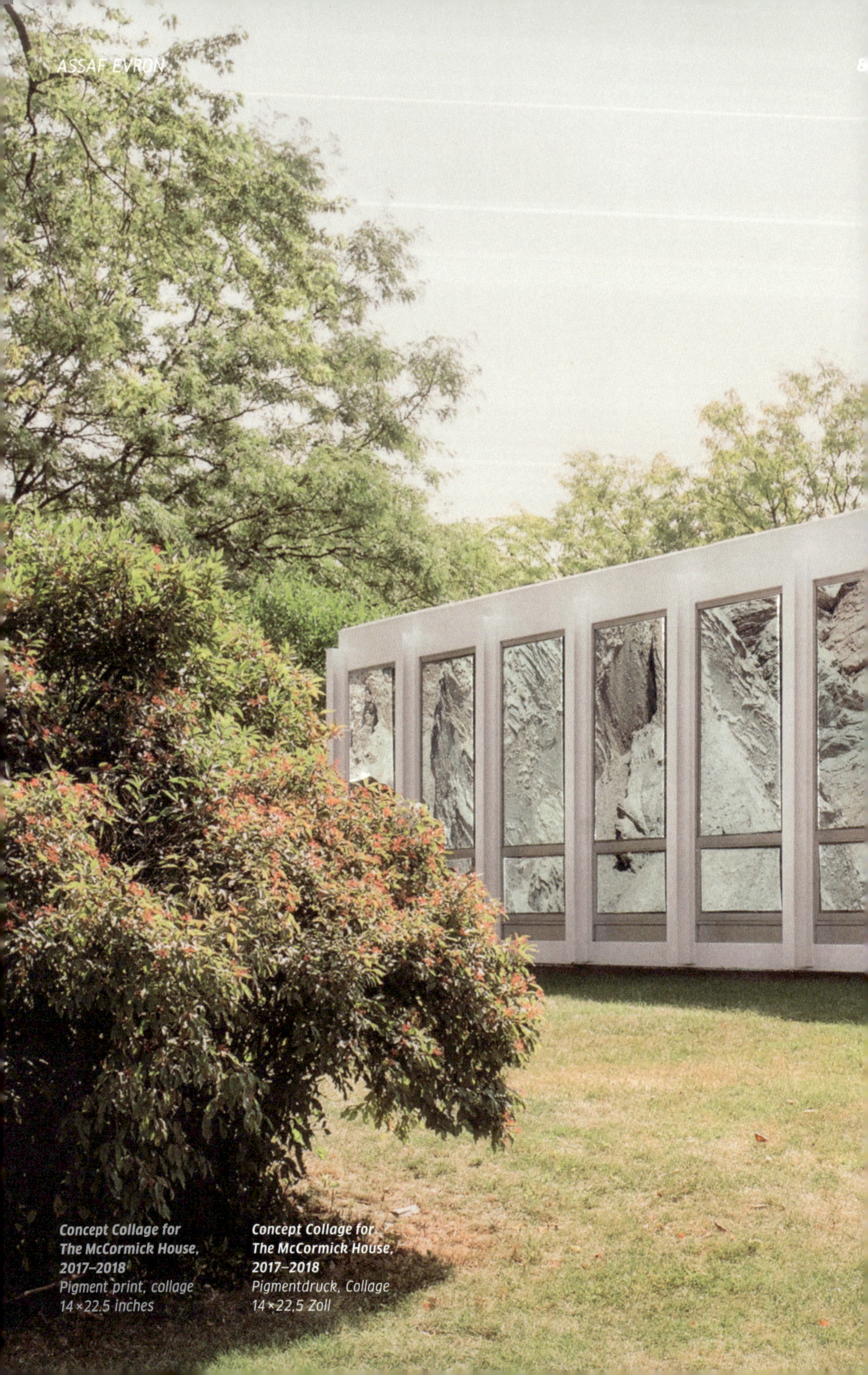

Concept Collage for The McCormick House, 2017–2018
Pigment print, collage
14 × 22.5 inches

Concept Collage for The McCormick House, 2017–2018
Pigmentdruck, Collage
14 × 22,5 Zoll

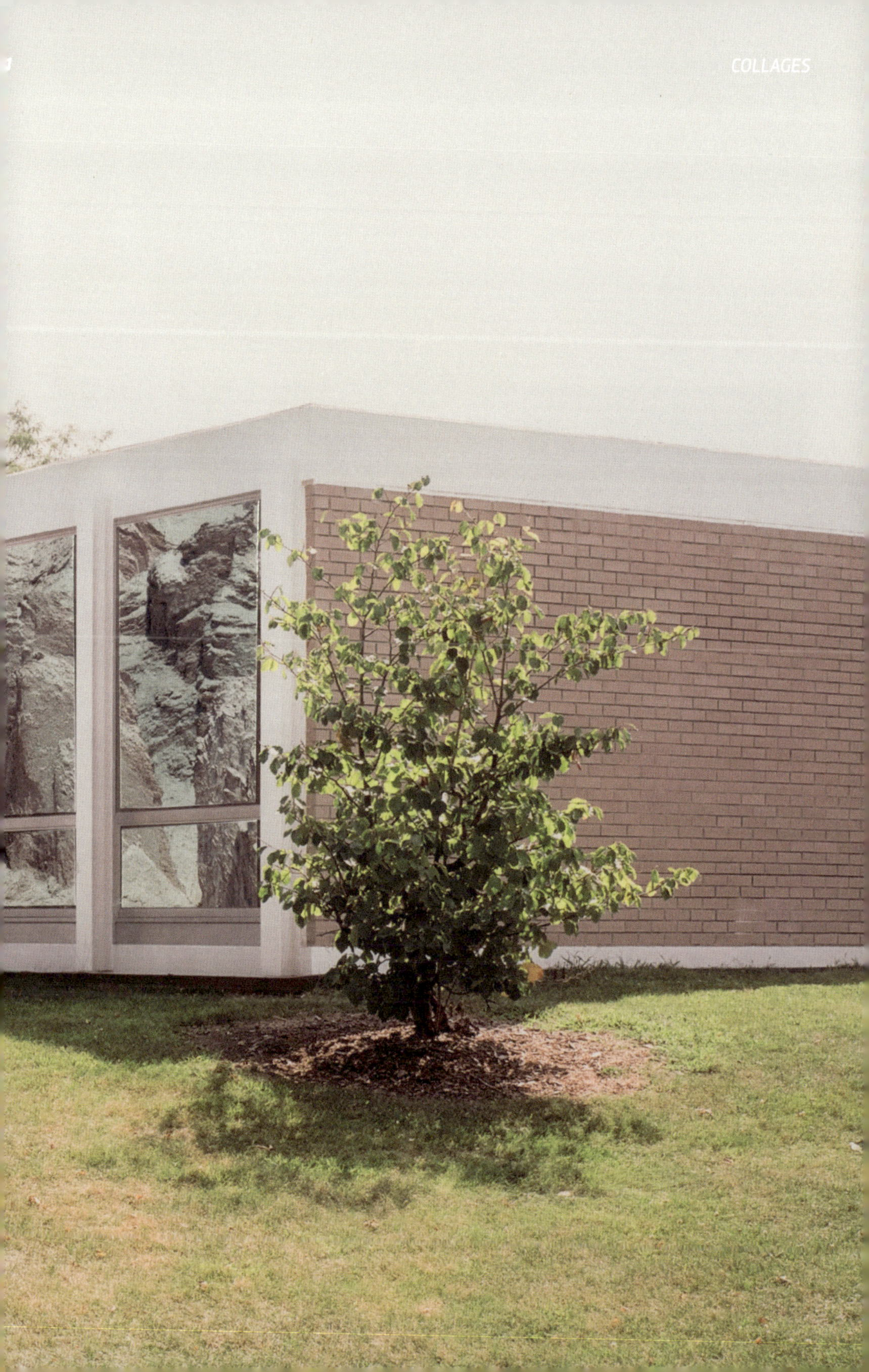

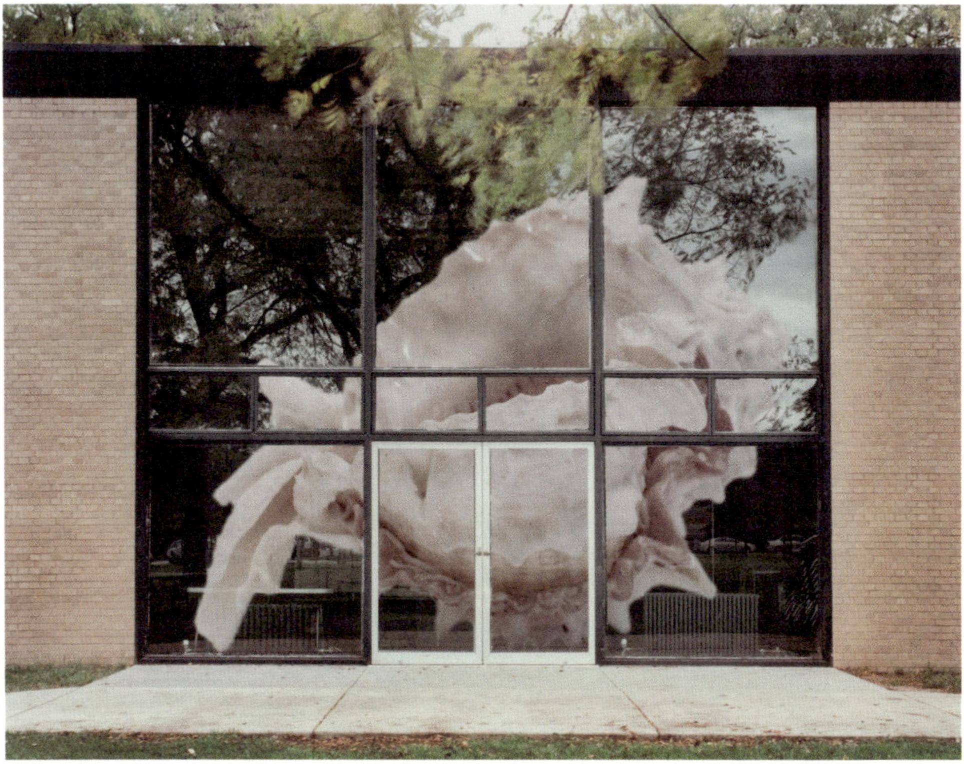

Concept Collage for The Robert F. Carr Memorial Chapel, 2017–2018
Pigment print, collage, 12 × 16 inches
Pp. 82–84

Concept Collage for The Robert F. Carr Memorial Chapel, 2017–2018
Pigmentdruck, Collage, 12 × 16 Zoll
S. 82–84

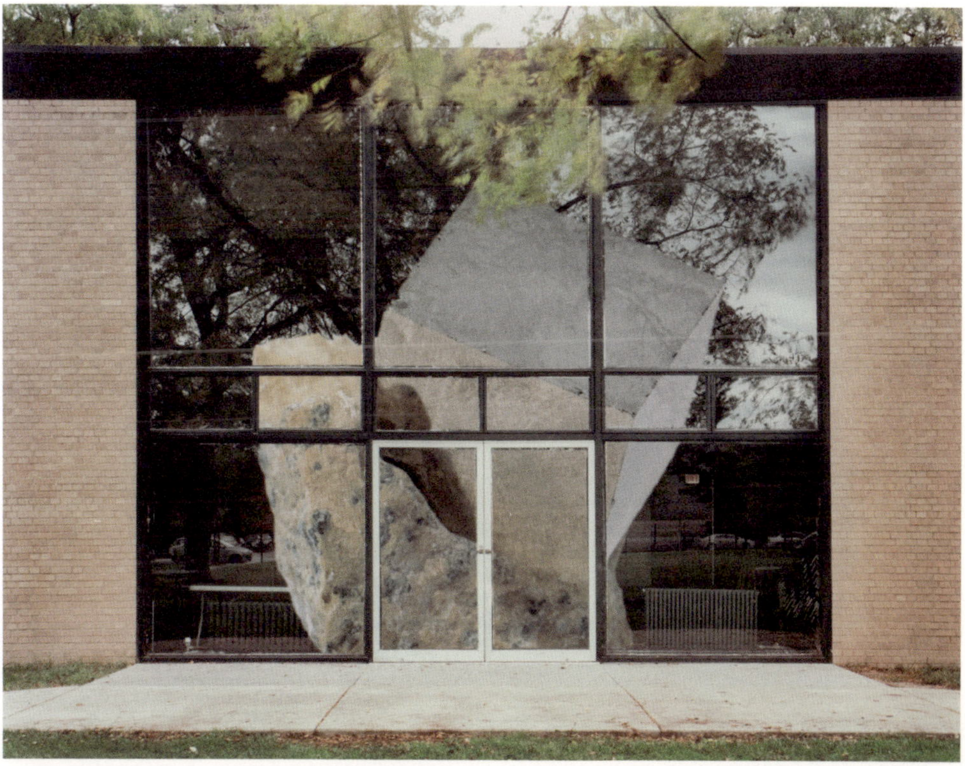

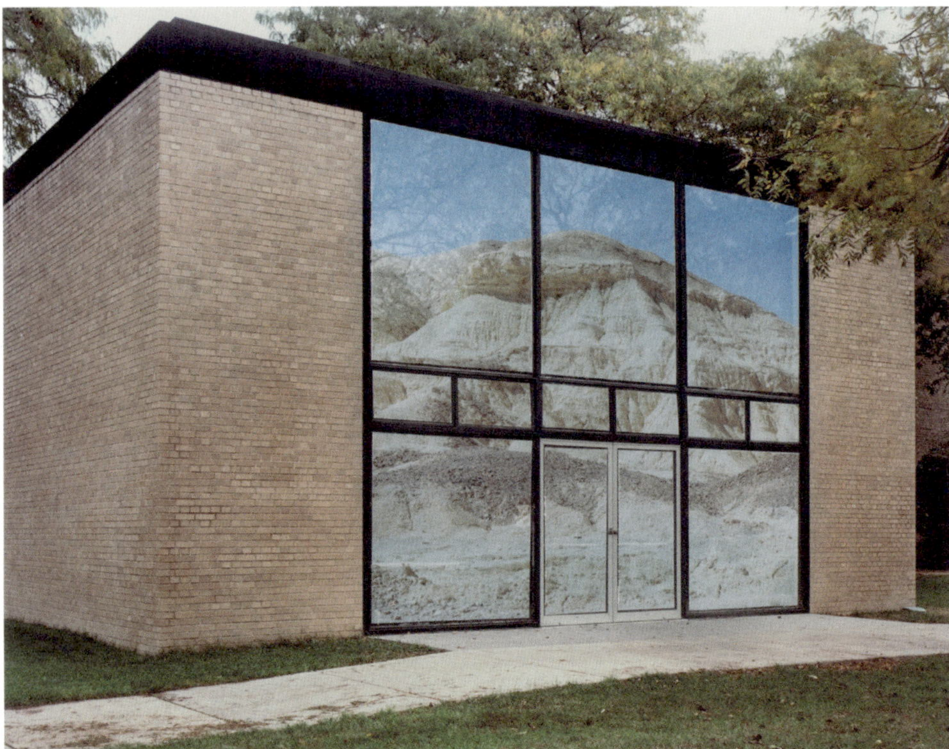

COLLAGES

Assaf Euron

The works in this series of photographic collages rethink Mies van der Rohe's collages in the context of his existing Midwest architectural projects. Euron's collages are studies in possible architectural interventions in Mies' buildings based on his own collage strategies. In his collages, Mies used photographs to represent landscape seen through the windows of his speculative grid-line architectures. The window modules thereby operate as a platform for photography, an idea which is the foundation of this project.

COLLAGEN

Assaf Euron

Die Fotocollagen dieser Reihe sind an die Collagen von Mies van der Rohe angelehnt und greifen dessen Architekturprojekte im Mittleren Westen auf. Euron untersucht in seinen Collagen potenzielle architektonische Interventionen an Mies van der Rohes Bauten und wendet dabei dessen eigene Collagentechnik an. Mies van der Rohe verwendete in seinen Collagen Fotografien, die den Blick auf die Landschaft durch die Fenster seiner erdachten Rasterlinienarchitektur darstellten. Die Fensterelemente dienten dabei als Plattform für die Fotografie. Der gleiche Gedanke liegt diesem Projekt zugrunde.

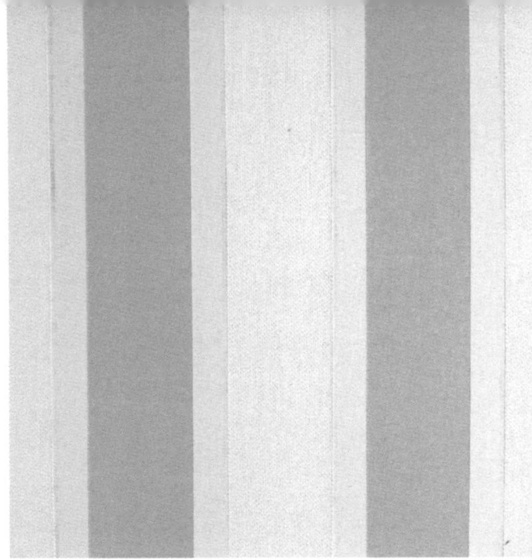

For many years, Serene Wise has been renting a studio in one of Chicago's oldest artists' residences on Michigan Avenue. One day she invited us to visit her. The Fine Arts Building, built in 1898, is like a time capsule of that era with operators running the wooden elevators, the sound of piano and violin students practicing and a sheet music business under the roof on the top floor.

*Serene Wise mietet in einem der ältesten Künstlerhäuser Chicagos, auf der Michigan Avenue, seit vielen Jahren ein Studio. Eines Tages lud sie uns zu sich ein. Das Fine Arts Building, gebaut 1898, ist wie aus der Zeit gefallen: Fahrstuhlführer, Fahrstühle aus Holz, man hört Klavier- und Geigenschüler*innen üben, und ganz oben unter dem Dach gibt es ein Geschäft für Notenblätter.*

SERENE WISE STUDIES IN GRAYS AND WHITE

Studies in Grays and White, 2013
Oil on cotton canvas on Masonite
24 × 24 inches
Pp. 88–93

Studies in Grays and White, 2013
Öl auf Baumwollleinwand, Masonit
24 × 24 Zoll
S. 88–93

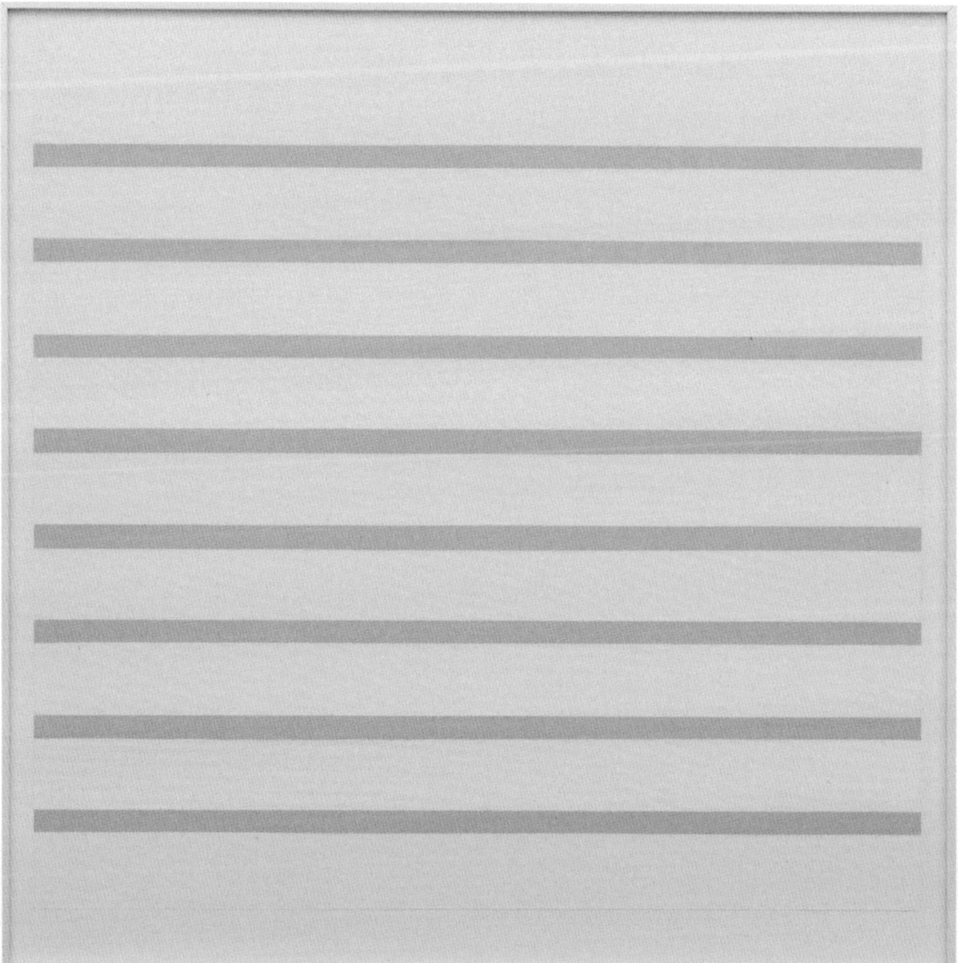

Summer I (Detail), 2005
Oil on cotton canvas on Masonite
24 × 24 inches

Summer I (Detail), 2005
Öl auf Baumwollleinwand, Masonit
24 × 24 Zoll

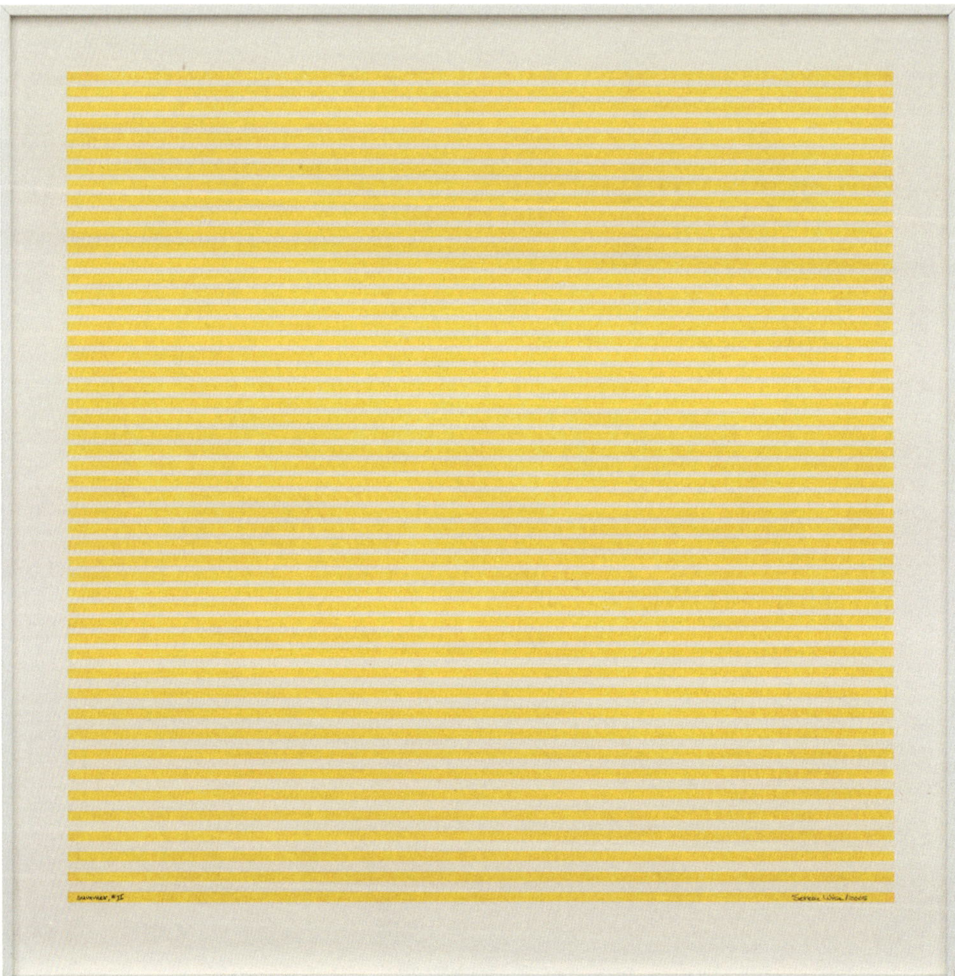

Summer I, 2005
Oil on cotton canvas on Masonite
24 × 24 inches

Summer I, 2005
Öl auf Baumwollleinwand, Masonit
24 × 24 Zoll

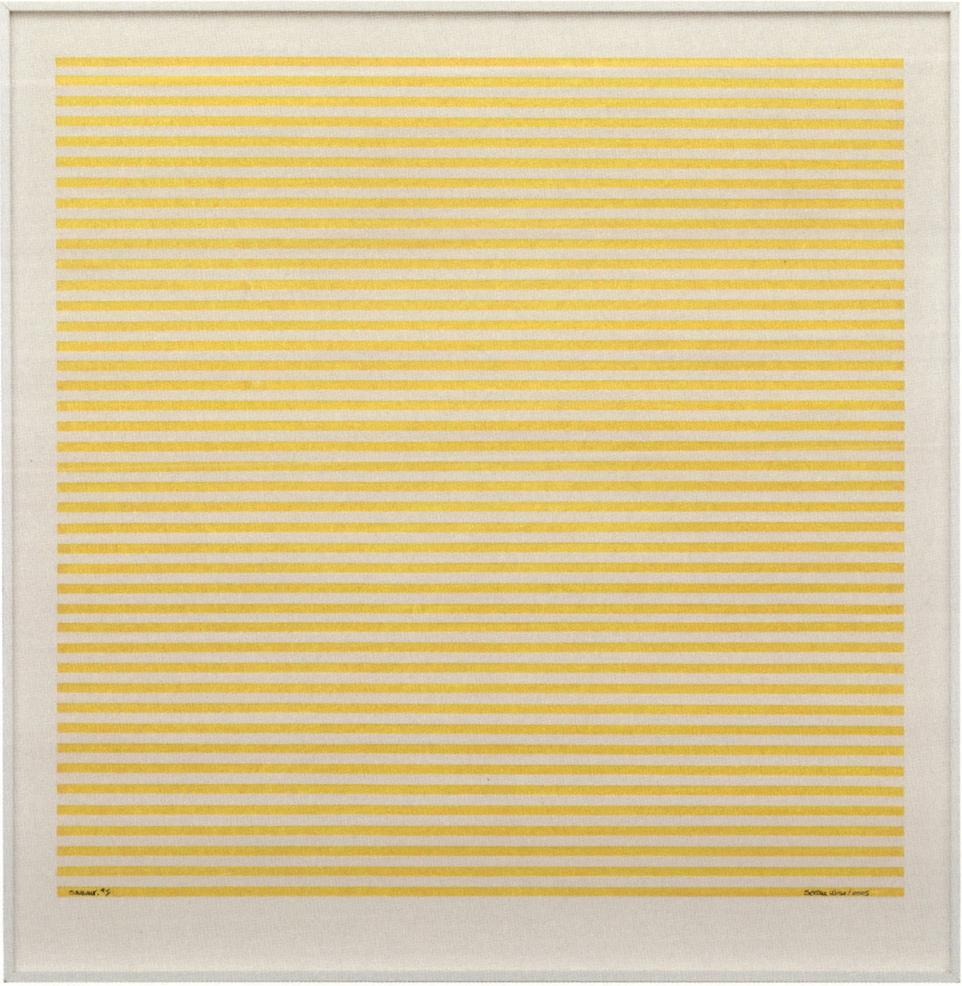

Summer II, 2005
Oil on cotton canvas on Masonite
24 × 24 inches

Summer II, 2005
Öl auf Baumwollleinwand, Masonit
24 × 24 Zoll

STUDIES IN GRAYS AND WHITE

Serene Wise

These paintings, Studies in Grays and White *reflect the teachings of three Bauhaus painters: the two Masters Johannes Itten (1888–1967) and Josef Albers (1888–1976), and a student, Max Bill (1908–1994). I am a painter. My work focuses on lines: I love lines, perhaps as Josef Albers loved the square. I am endlessly fascinated by the power and eloquence of lines and lines are my basic design elements. By applying oil on cotton canvas in a square format, I place lines over contrasting background fields and I use translucent and/or opaque textures such as the brushed line, the screened line, the sanded line, or a light wash of line.*

In this series, Studies in Grays and White *the grays are mixed from charcoal, chrome yellow, and titanium white. Here I investigate color values and color placements. The underpainting is either medium gray or very, very light gray and the overlay of lines is always screened oil.*

STUDIES IN GRAYS AND WHITE

Serene Wise

Die Arbeiten Studies in Grays and White *sind durch die Lehren dreier Maler der Bauhausbewegung geprägt: Johannes Itten (1888–1967), Josef Albers (1888–1976) und Max Bill (1908–1994). Ich bin Malerin. Linien spielen in meiner Arbeit eine zentrale Rolle: Ich mag Linien, vielleicht so, wie Josef Albers das Quadrat mochte. Ich bin unendlich fasziniert von der Kraft und Eloquenz von Linien, und Linien sind mein Hauptgestaltungselement.*

In meinen Ölarbeiten auf Baumwollleinwand im Quadratformat lege ich Linien über kontrastierende Hintergrundfelder. Dabei verwende ich durchschimmernde oder deckende Techniken, wie Pinselstrich, Rasterlinie, Texturlinie oder eine leichte Linienwaschung.

In dieser Reihe Studies in Grays and White *wurden die Grautöne aus Anthrazit, Chromgelb und Titanweiß gemischt. Ich beschäftige mich mit Farbwerten und Farbplatzierungen. Die Untermalung ist entweder in einem Mittelgrau oder sehr lichten Hellgrau gehalten und die darüber gelegten Linien sind immer in Öl gemalt.*

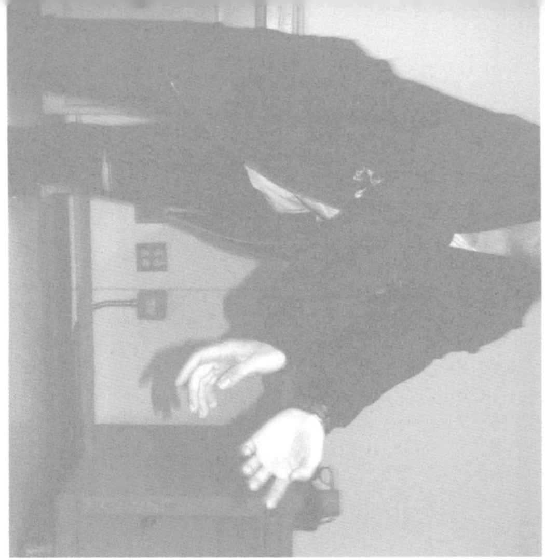

Heike Albrecht can be described as an all-rounder of the Berlin dance scene. She is a curator and dramaturge, comes from Werder near Potsdam, and lived in the Baumwollspinnerei in Leipzig in the 1990s when she invited the first international choreographers and dancers there. Albrecht became our second resident in the summer of 2018.

Heike Albrecht kann man als eine Allrounderin der Berliner Tanzszene bezeichnen. Sie ist Kuratorin und Dramaturgin, kommt aus Werder bei Potsdam, lebte in den 1990er-Jahren in der Baumwollspinnerei in Leipzig, als sie die ersten internationalen Choreografen und Tänzer dorthin einlud. Albrecht wurde unsere zweite Residentin im Sommer 2018.

HEIKE ALBRECHT
RESIDENZ / SPURENBEWEGUNG

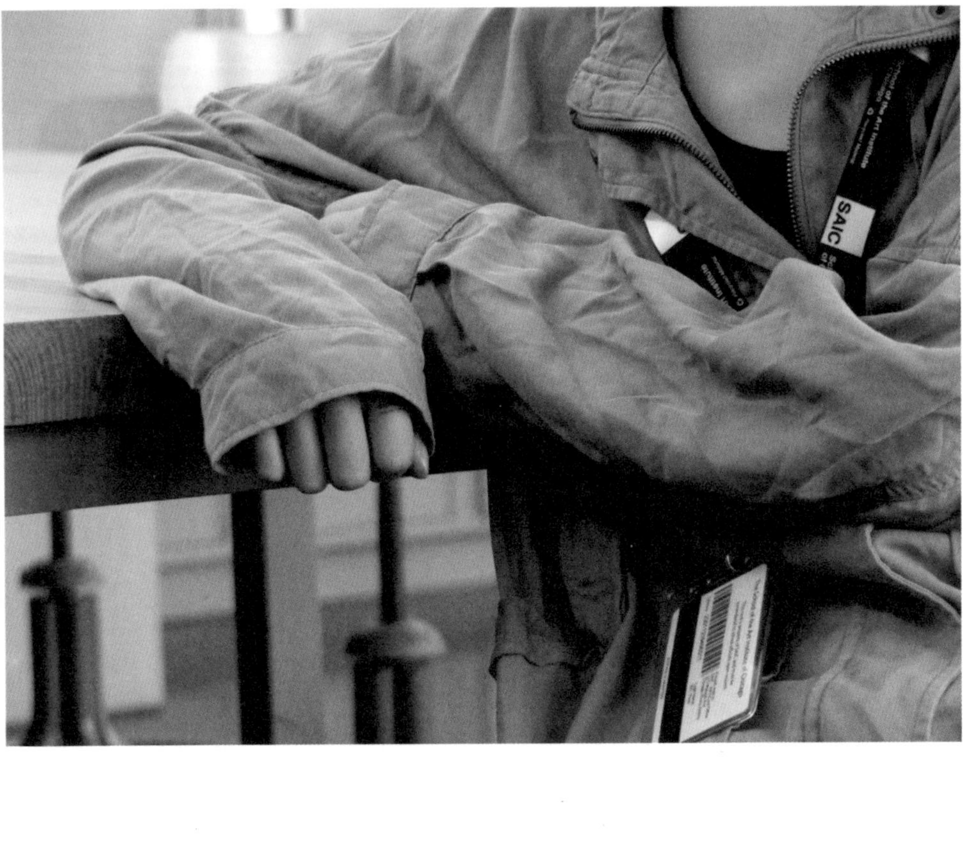

Trace Movement (detail), 2018
SAIC_Fashion, Body and Garment
Pp. 102–109

Spurenbewegung (Detail), 2018
SAIC_Fashion, Body and Garment
S. 102–109

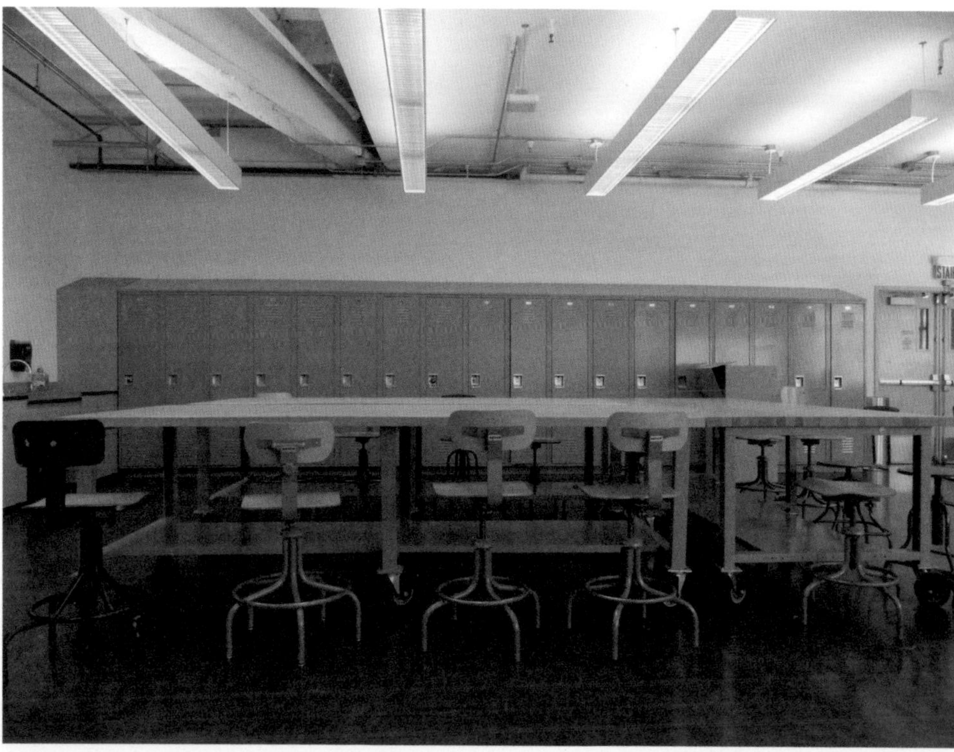
STAIRS

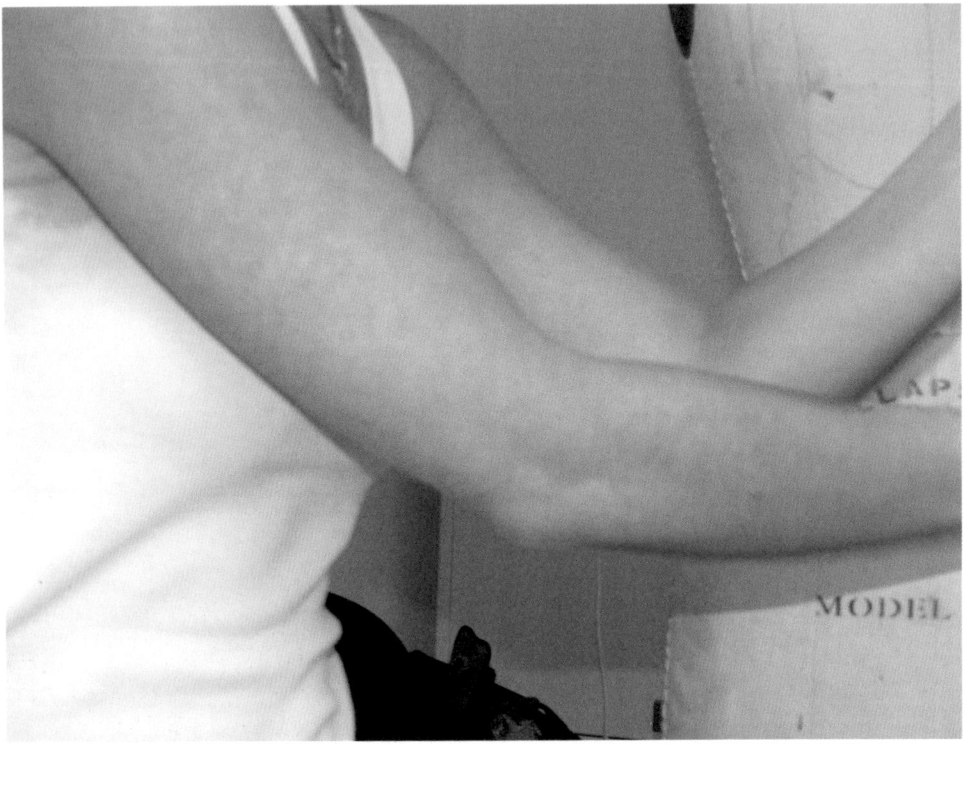
MODEL

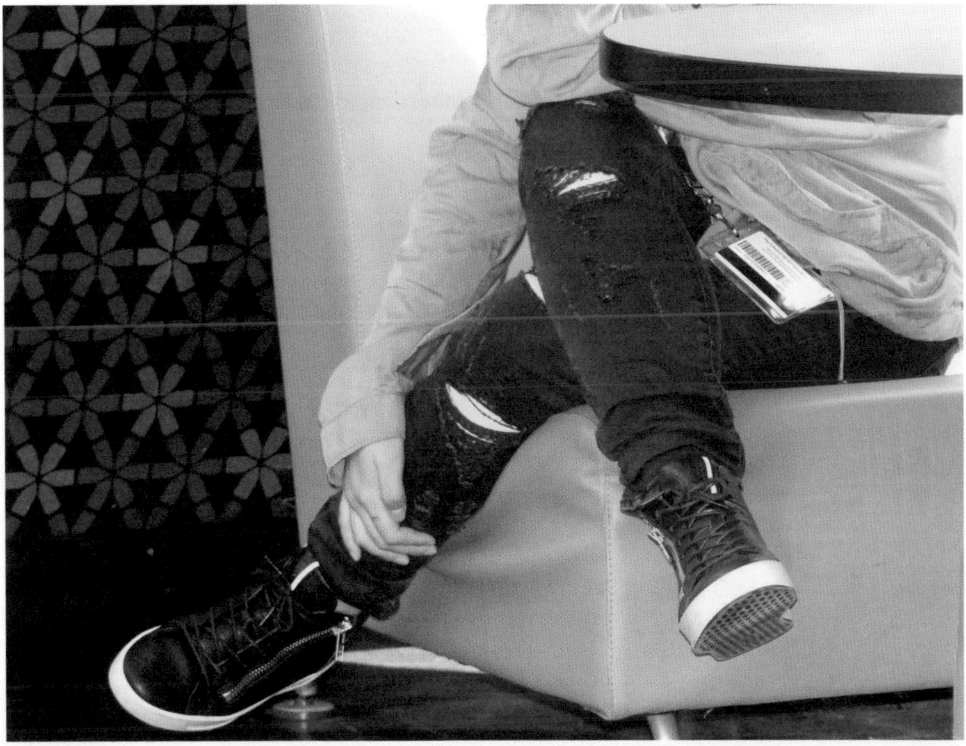

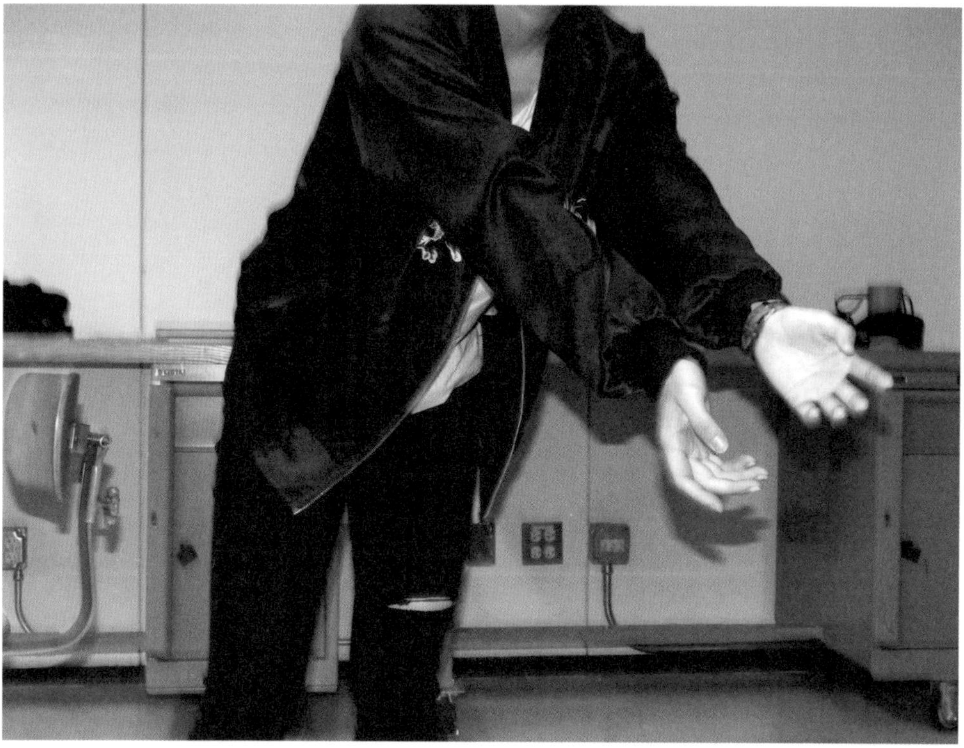

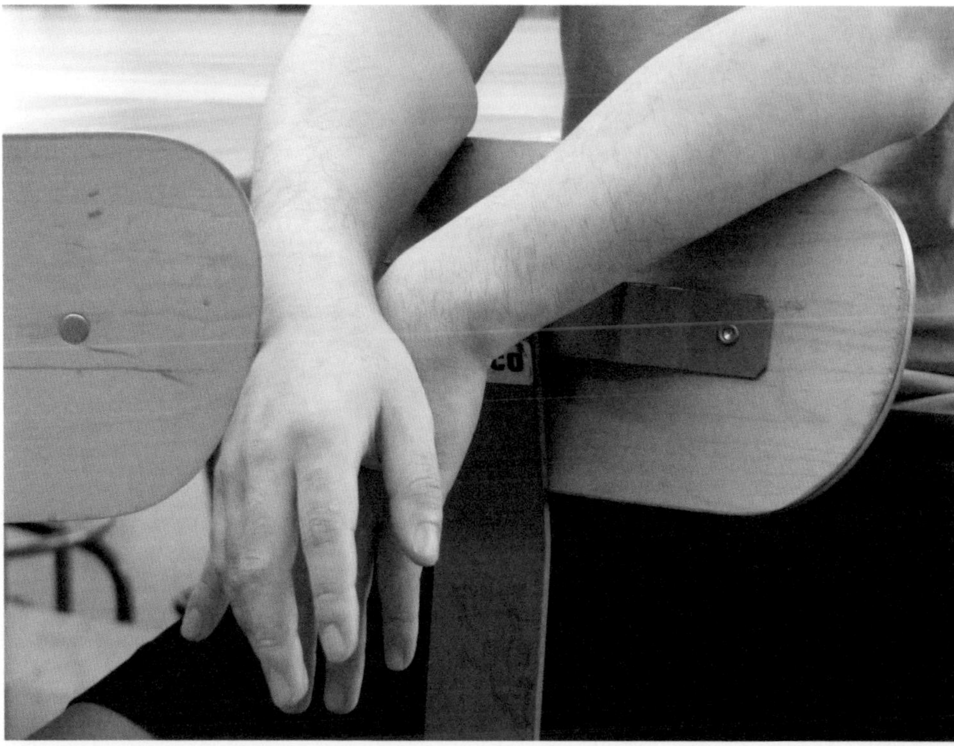

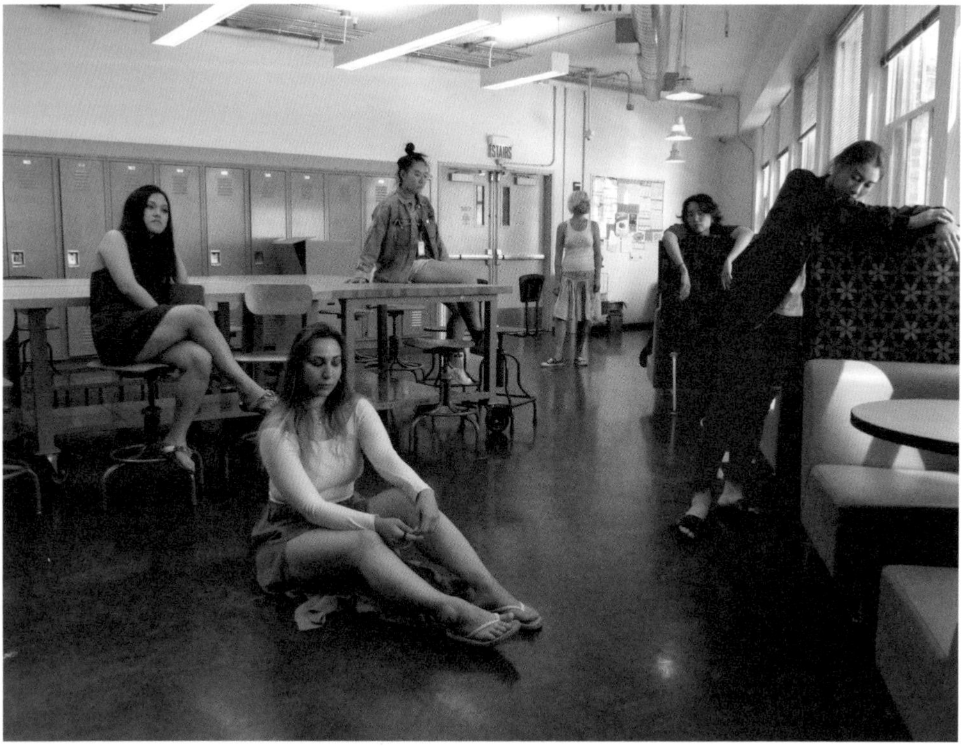
STAIRS

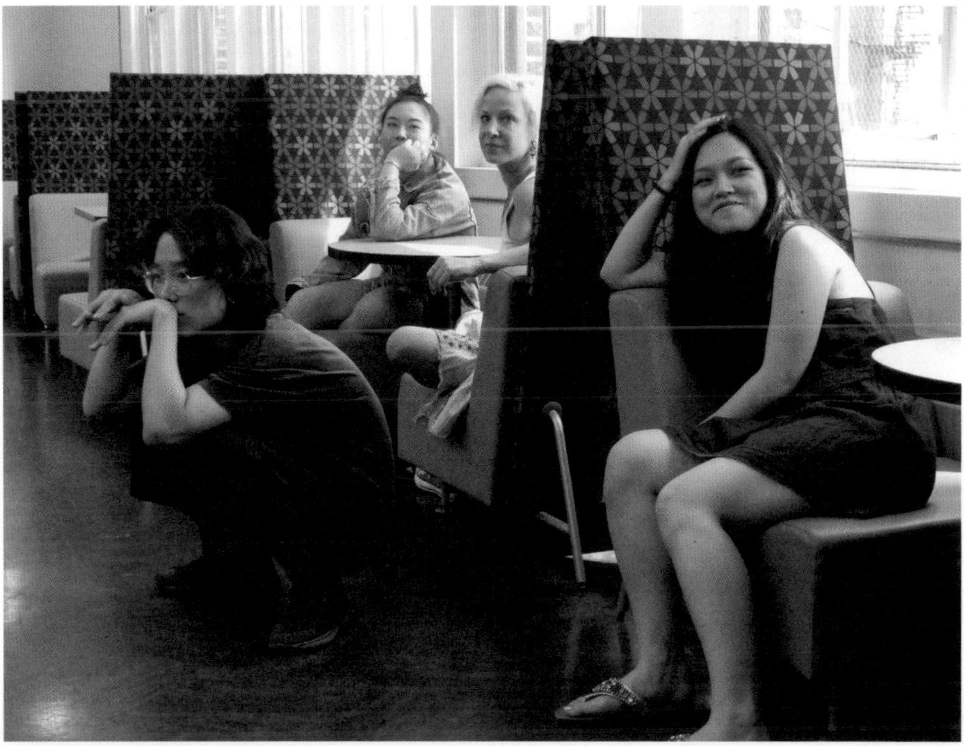

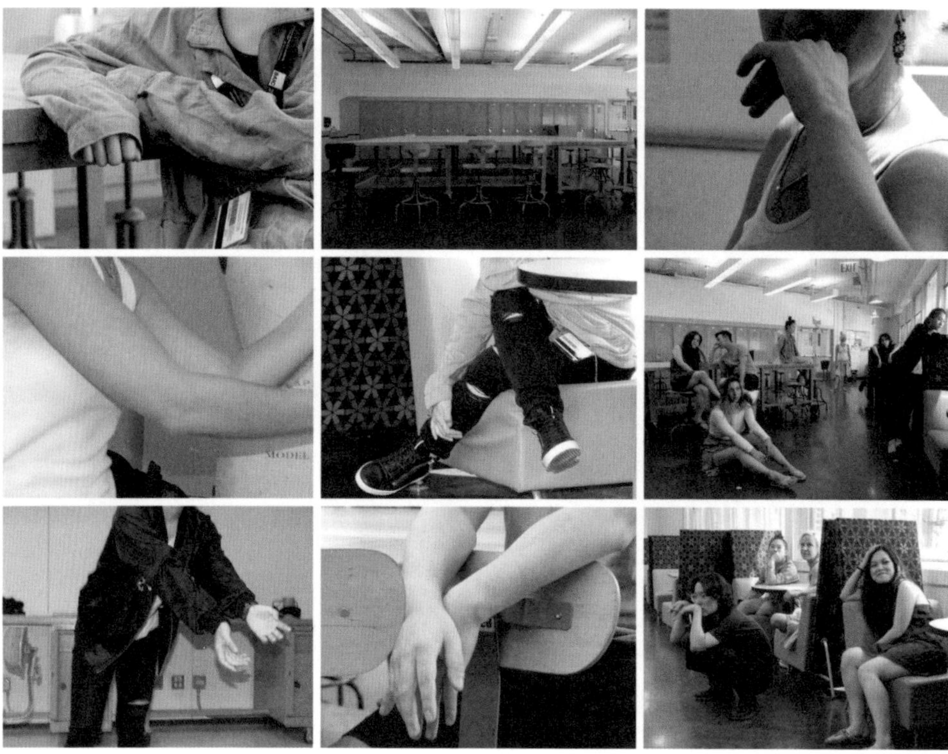

Trace Movement, collage, 2018
Foyer Goethe-Institut Chicago
ca. 98.4 × 157.5 inches

Spurenbewegung, Collage, 2018
Foyer Goethe-Institut Chicago
ca. 98,4 × 157,5 Zoll

TRACE MOVEMENT

Heike Albrecht

At the beginning of the 20th century, modern dance advanced to become a new and formative art form and played a pivotal role on stage at the Bauhaus. Oskar Schlemmer's dramaturgical theory, in which the relationship of man and space was at the forefront, is exemplary. In his teachings, he synergistically combined kinetic movement studies, figurative illustration and philosophy, placing the close interaction in the artistic work and the human body at the center of his work. Schlemmer defined his elementary obsession to observe people and their movements.

In my lecture Movement Traces *at the Fashion, Body and Garment Department of the School of the Art Institute of Chicago, directed by Anke Loh and Liat Smestad, I related Schlemmer's theories and his work on the* Triadisches Ballett *of 1912 to current developments in body image and movement research in contemporary dance and performance. The result is a photo series involving the participants of the Post-Baccalaureate Certificate (Summer Bootcamp): Ann Stahl, Jue Wang, Mengyi Qin, Danielle F Grouse, Meilun He, Yuxuan Chen, Yiwei Wu, Junqi Qu.*

SPURENBEWEGUNG

Heike Albrecht

Anfang des 20. Jahrhunderts avancierte der moderne Tanz zu einer so neuen wie prägenden Kunstform und bestimmte maßgeblich das Bühnengeschehen am Bauhaus. Beispielgebend sind das Werk von Oskar Schlemmer sowie seine Bühnentheorie, in der die Beziehung des Menschen zum Raum im Vordergrund stand. In seiner Lehre führte er kinetische Bewegungsstudien, figurative Illustrationen und Philosophie synergetisch zusammen und stellte die engen Wechselbeziehungen innerhalb der künstlerischen Arbeit und dem menschlichen Körper in den Mittelpunkt seines Wirkens. Diese elementare Obsession, Menschen und deren Bewegung zu folgen, ist es, was die Arbeit Schlemmers definiert.

In dem Vortrag Trace Movement *am Studiengang* Fashion – Body and Garment *an der School of the Art Institute of Chicago, geleitet von Anke Loh und Liat Smestad, stellte Heike Albrecht Schlemmers Theorien und seine Arbeit zum* Triadischen Ballett *von 1912 in Beziehung zu aktuellen europäischen Entwicklungen der Körperbild- und Bewegungsforschung im zeitgenössischen Tanz und in der Performance. Entstanden ist dabei eine Fotoreihe unter der Mitwirkung der Teilnehmer*innen des Post-Baccalaureate Certificate (Summer Bootcamp): Ann Stahl, Jue Wang, Mengyi Qin, Danielle F Grouse, Meilun He, Yuxuan Chen, Yiwei Wu, Junqi Qu.*

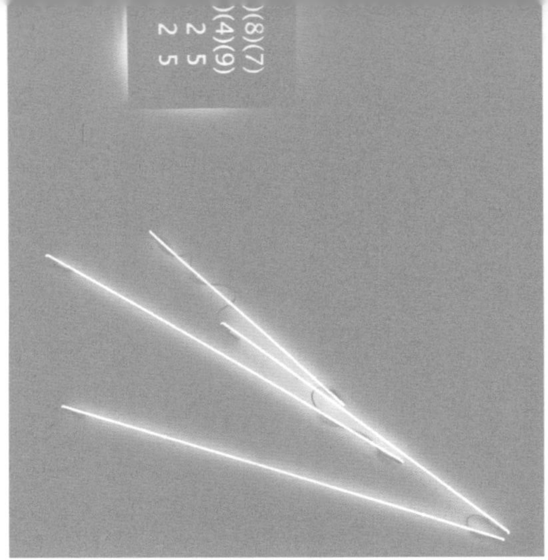

Monika Wulfers visited the Goethe-Institut on our Open Day. We entered into a conversation and the artist began to tell stories: She emigrated from Berlin to Chicago in the 1960s, studied Painting and Film at the School of the Art Institute of Chicago, then lived on an island on Lake Michigan, where she campaigned for environmental protection. Her installations brought light into our dark corridors.

Monika Wulfers besuchte das Goethe-Institut an einem Tag der offenen Tür. Wir kamen ins Gespräch: In den 1960er-Jahren ist Monika Wulfers von Berlin nach Chicago ausgewandert, hat Malerei und Film an der School of the Art Institute Chicago studiert, danach auf einer Insel im Michigansee gelebt und dort für den Umweltschutz gekämpft. Ihre Installation brachte Licht in unsere dunklen Flure.

MONIKA WULFERS
LINES AND NUMBERS

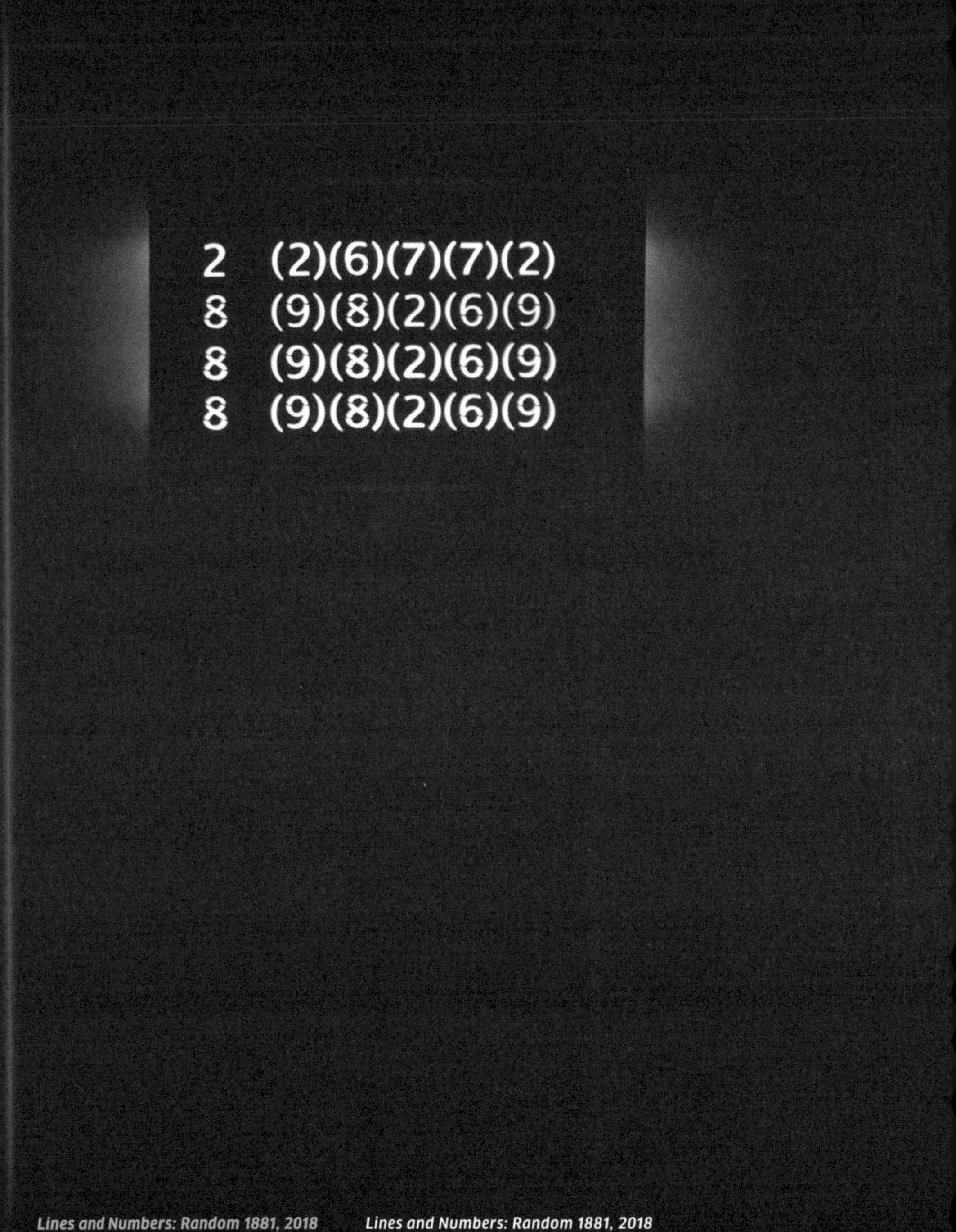

Lines and Numbers: Random 1881, 2018
Argon, glass tubes, transformers, wiring, steel plate
LED lights: 80 × 103 × 2.5 inches
Numbers: 24 × 38 inches

Lines and Numbers: Random 1881, 2018
Argon, Glasrohre, Transformatoren, Verkabelung, Stahlplatte
LED-Leuchten: 80 × 103 × 103 × 2,5 Zoll
Zahlen: 24 × 38 Zoll

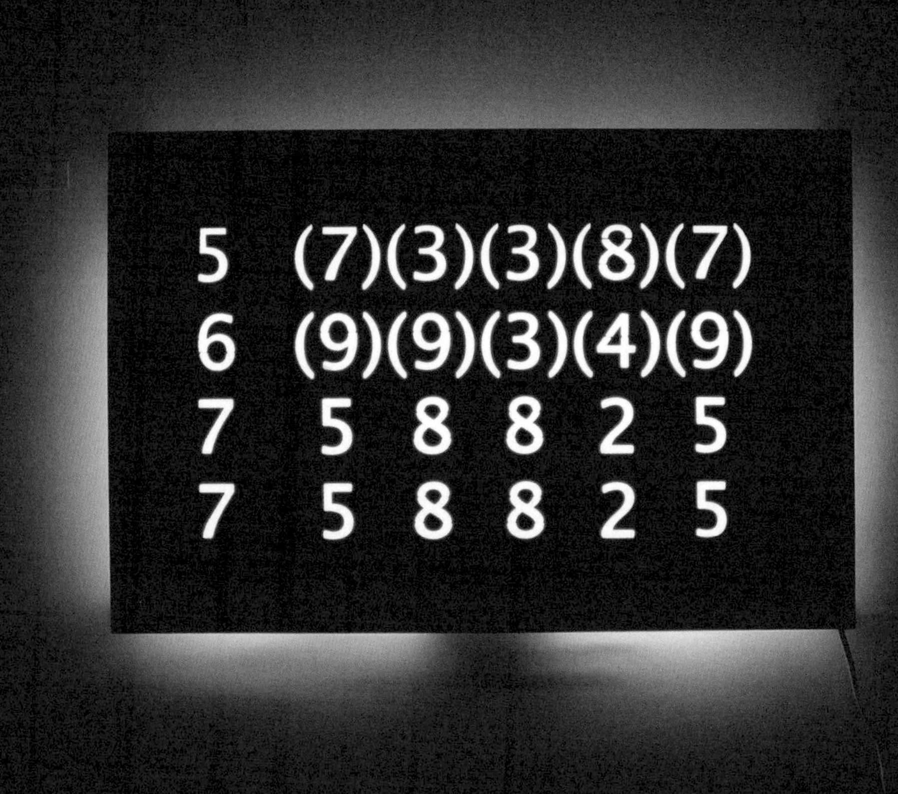

Lines and Numbers: Random 5677, 2018
Argon, glass tubes, variable length,
transformers, wiring, steel plate
LED lights: 88 × 48 × 2.5 inches
Numbers: 24 × 38 inches

Lines and Numbers: Random 5677, 2018
Argon, Glasrohre, variable Länge,
Transformatoren, Verkabelung, Stahlplatte
LED-Leuchten: 88 × 48 × 2,5 Zoll
Zahlen: 24 × 38 Zoll

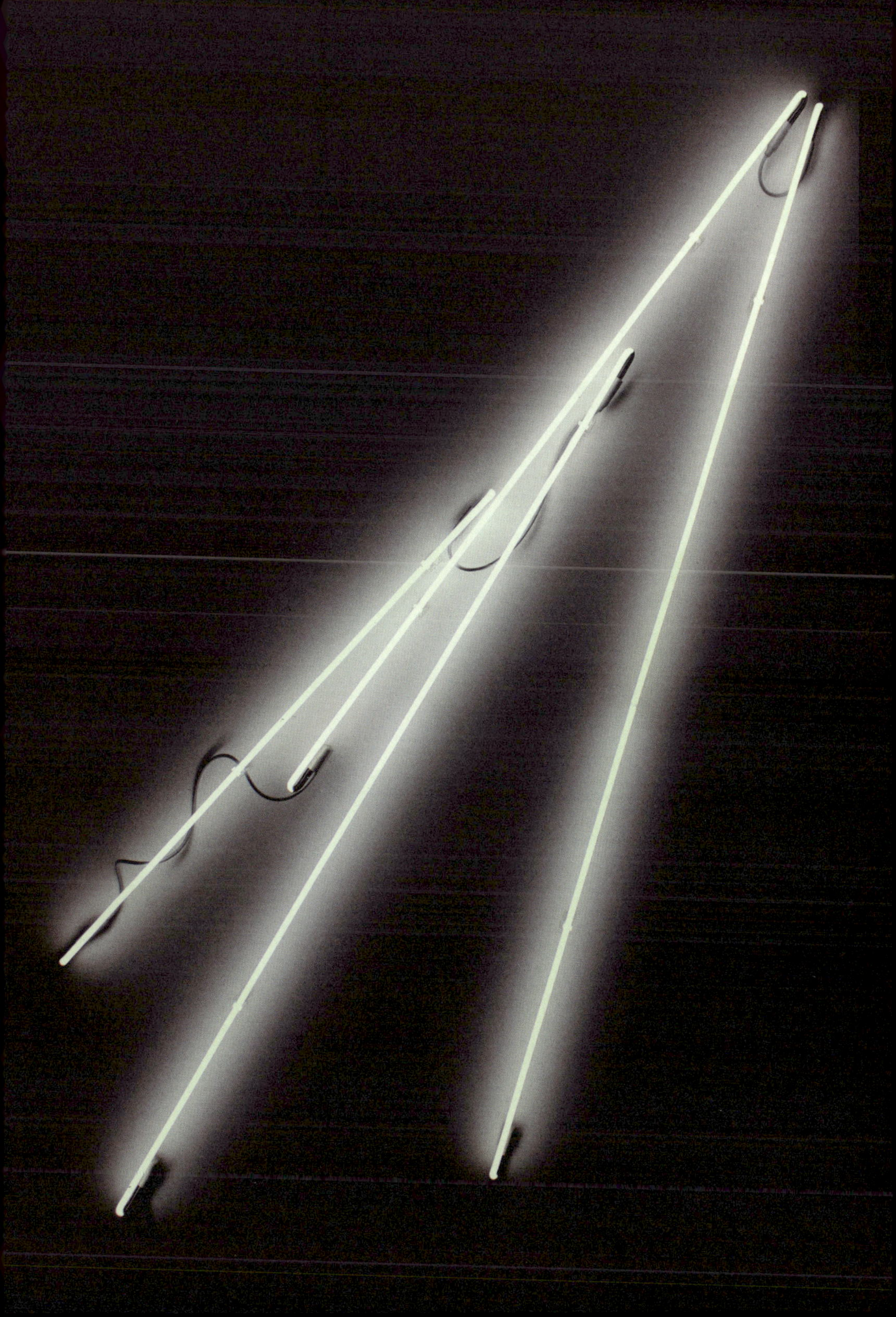

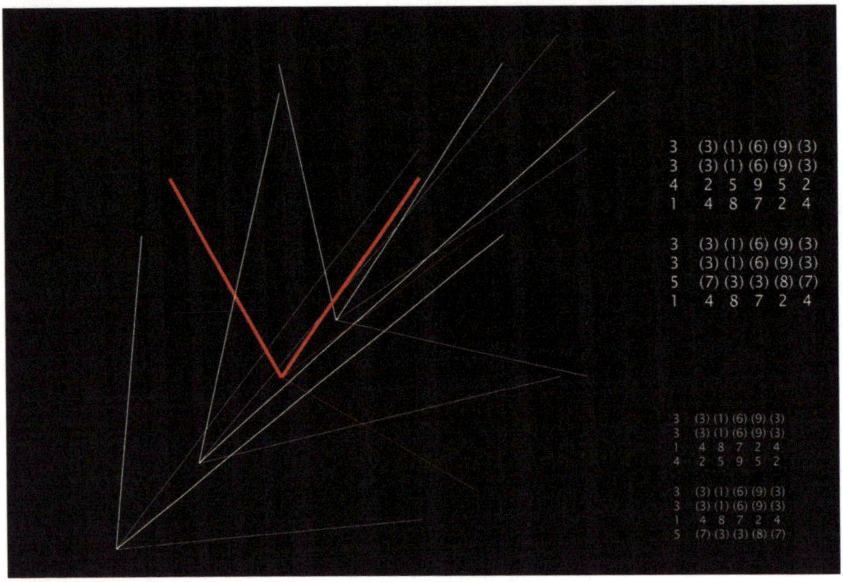

Random 3341 3351, 2018
Digital print on Hahnemühle Photo Rag
20 × 30 inches

Random 3341 3351, 2018
Digitaldruck auf Hahnemühle Photo Rag
20 × 30 Zoll

LINES AND NUMBERS

Anne Rorimer
Art Historian, Introduction to the exhibition catalog, published by the Goethe-Institut Chicago, 1979

Straight vertical, horizontal, and diagonal lines are based on invisible outlines, which generate values to determine any number of lines and their location in a composition. This body of work is collectively titled Random 1111 8888.

Numbers in the form of matrices, which are patterns in their own right, define the location of these lines on a grid. In Random 3341 3351, lines mirror each other. Their corresponding values are reflected in the 3314/41 3315/51 reversed orders of the number lines. The matrices and their signifiers, 1 through 8, here 1, 3, 4, 5 become the titles of the work.

LINIEN UND ZAHLEN

Anne Rorimer
Kunsthistorikerin, Einleitung zum Ausstellungskatalog, Herausgeber Goethe-Institut Chicago, 1979

Gerade vertikale, horizontale und diagonale Linien basieren auf unsichtbaren Konturen, die Werte erzeugen, aus denen eine zufällige Anzahl von Linien und deren Anordnung in einer Komposition bestimmt wird. Das Gesamtwerk trägt den Titel Random 1111 8888.

Zahlen in der Form von Matrizen, die für sich selbst genommen Muster sind, bestimmen die Anordnung dieser Linien in einem Raster. Random 3341 3351 beinhaltet eine spiegelbildliche Anordnung von Linien. Ihre korrespondierenden Werte zeigen sich in den umgekehrten Reihenfolgen der Zahlenlinien 3314/41 3315/51. Aus den Matrizen und ihren signifikanten Stellen 1 bis 8, hier 1, 3, 4, 5, entstehen die Titel der Arbeit.

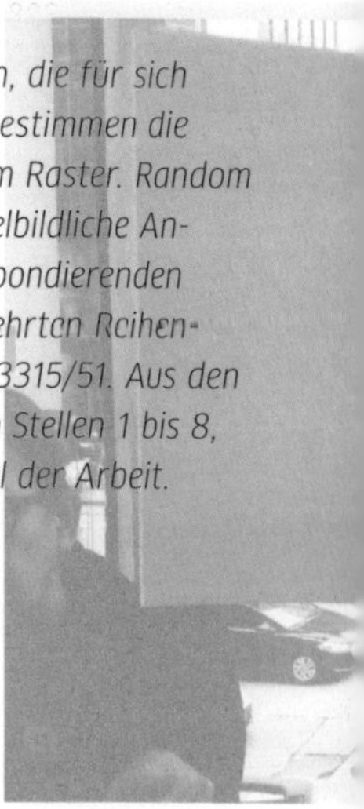

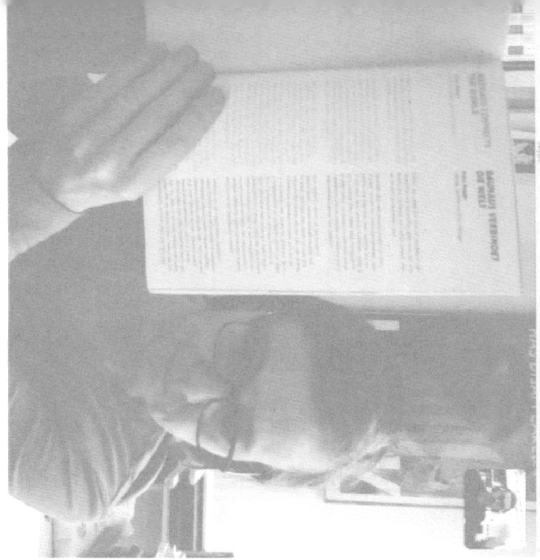

Fragments. Openness. Visualizing structures and processes. Materials: Fabric and metal. Reference to weaving. Interweaving. Connecting. Organic. Human. Weaving, building and constructing. Memories. Fading. Size. Small, compact, little piece.

Fragmente. Offenheit. Strukturen und Prozesse sichtbar machen. Materialien: Stoff und Metall. Bezug zum Weben. Verweben. Verbinden. Organisch. Human. Weben, bauen und konstruieren. Erinnerungen. Verblassen. Größe. Klein, kompakt, kleine Stücke.

BAUHAUS ESSAYS
TEXTE ZUM BAUHAUS

BAUHAUS BEYOND BORDERS: GERMAN INFLUENCES ON THE CHICAGO SKYLINE

Ingrid Zeller

Skyscrapers, curtain walls, glass towers, steel structures – Chicago is world-renowned for its innovative and modern architecture. In the course of the 20th century, the city's skyline was shaped significantly by ideas from the Bauhaus School, which was founded in 1919 in Weimar, Germany, and existed in Germany until 1933. 2019 marks the 100th anniversary of the Bauhaus.

The Bauhaus mission was to create products that were not only innovative, practical, and affordable, but also set a superb aesthetic standard, adjusted to an industrialized society. Although architecture was the school's primary focus, many other items including furniture and household articles enjoyed groundbreaking designs, while painting, music, and dance were taken in new directions by artists Wassily Kandinsky, Paul Klee, and Oskar Schlemmer, among many others. Bauhaus products came to represent a modern image that was typically linear, functional, aesthetically pleasing, lacking traditional ornamentation, and featuring the use of industrial materials.

After the National Socialists seized power in 1933, the Bauhaus was closed; many Bauhaus artists emigrated and carried on their work in other parts of the world. In addition to Tel Aviv, Chicago is considered one of the cities that demonstrate and have promoted most strikingly the extraordinary influence of the Bauhaus. Of the Bauhaus artists who relocated to the USA, Walter Gropius became a professor at Harvard University, Annie and Josef Albers taught at Black Mountain College, and Ludwig Mies van der Rohe became the director of the Illinois Institute of Technology (Armour Institute) in Chicago.

BAUHAUS BEYOND BORDERS: DEUTSCHE EINFLÜSSE AUF DIE SKYLINE VON CHICAGO

Ingrid Zeller

Wolkenkratzer, Vorhangfassaden, Glastürme, Stahlkonstruktionen – Chicago ist weltweit bekannt für seine innovative und moderne Architektur. Die Skyline der Stadt wurde im Lauf des 20. Jahrhunderts maßgeblich durch das Gedankengut des 1919 in Weimar gegründeten Staatlichen Bauhauses geprägt, das in Deutschland bis 1933 Bestand hatte. 2019 feiert das Bauhaus sein 100-jähriges Bestehen.

Ziel der Kunstschule war die Entwicklung von innovativen, praktischen und bezahlbaren Produkten. Diese setzten höchste ästhetische Maßstäbe und entsprachen damit den Anforderungen einer industrialisierten Gesellschaft. Der Schwerpunkt des Bauhauses lag im Bereich Architektur, doch das richtungsweisende Design prägte darüber hinaus viele andere Produkte wie Möbel und Haushaltsartikel. Durch Künstler wie Wassily Kandinsky, Paul Klee und Oskar Schlemmer erfuhren auch Bereiche wie Malerei, Musik und Tanz eine neue Ausrichtung. Bauhausprodukte wurden zum Inbegriff moderner Gestaltung – geradlinig, funktional, ästhetisch, schnörkellos – und zeigten den charakteristischen Einsatz industrieller Materialien.

Neben Tel Aviv gilt Chicago als eine der Städte, in denen der bemerkenswerte Einfluss des Bauhauses und die weitere Umsetzung seiner Ideen besonders deutlich ablesbar sind.

Nach der Machtübernahme der Nationalsozialisten 1933 wurde das Bauhaus geschlossen, viele Bauhauskünstler wanderten aus und setzten ihre Arbeit in anderen Teilen der Welt fort. Neben Tel Aviv gilt Chicago als eine der Städte, in denen der bemerkenswerte Einfluss des Bauhauses und die weitere Umsetzung seiner Ideen beson-

In 1937, the former Bauhaus Master László Moholy-Nagy founded the New Bauhaus School of Design in Chicago, the only institute that formally continued the course of study that had been established in the German Bauhaus. Moholy-Nagy directed the institute, soon called School of Design, until his death in 1946. Light, publicity, photography, and machine learning were emphasized even more strongly under his leadership, as were connections to the sciences. Today, the Institute of Design is part of the IIT (Illinois Institute of Technology).

LUDWIG MIES VAN DER ROHE DESIGNED THE ENTIRE CAMPUS OF THE IIT AS WELL AS MANY OTHER ICONIC BUILDINGS IN CHICAGO AND WORLDWIDE.

Among the most prominent and influential architects to emerge from the Bauhaus and to shape the image of the city of Chicago was the architect Ludwig Mies van der Rohe (1886–1969). He designed the entire campus of the IIT as well as many other iconic buildings in Chicago and worldwide and trained generations of young architects. Particularly representative for Miesian architecture in the Chicago area are S. R. Crown Hall at the IIT, the Lake Shore Drive Apartments, the IBM Building (today AMA), Federal Center Plaza, One Illinois Center, McCormick House in Elmhurst, and Farnsworth House in Plano. The famous motto "less is more" genuinely captures the architect's minimalist approach that also highlighted the industrial essence of a building as a central and visible element of the construction process. Mies believed that "God is in the detail." He devised "I-beams" to liven up his buildings' façades, covered his buildings with curtain walls, and invented the concept of "universal space" – a large space in a building that is unobstructed and thus conducive to individual planning by tenants.

THE CHICAGO SKYLINE WOULD BE UNTHINKABLE WITHOUT THE INFLUENCES OF THE MID-CENTURY MODERN STYLE.

This International Style, now called Mid-Century Modern Style, of which Mies is considered a

ders deutlich ablesbar sind. Zu den in die USA emigrierten Bauhauskünstlern gehören Walter Gropius, der eine Professur an der Harvard University antrat, Annie und Josef Albers, die am Black Mountain College lehrten, und Ludwig Mies van der Rohe, der Direktor des Illinois Institute of Technology (Armour Institute) in Chicago wurde.

1937 gründete der ehemalige Bauhausmeister László Moholy-Nagy das New Bauhaus, die einzige Hochschule, die den am deutschen Bauhaus eingerichteten Studiengang formell weiterführte. Moholy-Nagy leitete das bald als School of Design bezeichnete Institut bis zu seinem Tod im Jahr 1946. Beleuchtung, Werbedesign, Fotografie und maschinelles Lernen erfuhren unter seiner Leitung eine noch stärkere Schwerpunktsetzung, ebenso wie die Verbindung zur Wissenschaft. Heute ist das Institute of Design Teil des IIT (Illinois Institute of Technology).

VON LUDWIG MIES VAN DER ROHE STAMMT DER ENTWURF DES GESAMTEN IIT-CAMPUS WIE AUCH VIELER ANDERER IKONISCHER BAUTEN IN CHICAGO UND WELTWEIT.

Zu den bekanntesten und einflussreichsten Architekten, die aus der Bauhausbewegung hervorgingen und das Bild der Stadt Chicago prägten, zählt der Architekt Ludwig Mies van der Rohe. Von ihm stammt der Entwurf des gesamten IIT-Campus wie auch vieler anderer ikonischer Bauten in Chicago und weltweit. Er schulte ganze Generationen junger Architekten. Zu den bedeutendsten Beispielen seiner Architektur gehören die S. R. Crown Hall am IIT, die Lake Shore Drive Apartments, das IBM-Gebäude (heute AMA), die Federal Center Plaza, das One Illinois Center, das McCormick House in Elmhurst und das Farnsworth House in Plano. Sein berühmtes Motto „Weniger ist mehr" bringt den minimalistischen Ansatz des Architekten treffend zum Ausdruck, bei dem gleichzeitig die industrielle Essenz eines Gebäudes als zentrales, sichtbares Element des Bauprozesses im Vordergrund stand. Mies van der Rohe vertrat den Standpunkt, dass „Gott im Detail steckt". Er setzte Doppel-T-Träger als Gestaltungselement seiner Fassaden

founder together with Gropius and Le Corbusier, advocated an industrial and impersonal focus that, along with its international orientation, was soon embraced worldwide. The aesthetic elements of modern architecture, including the departure from traditional ornamentation, the use of grid-like patterns, and the integration of modular rather than symmetrical units, exerted an immense influence on the development of architecture in the USA. The result was a focus on an honest, open approach that showcased the building's structure, for example its steel skeleton, and featured materials such as steel, glass, concrete, or granite. The Chicago Skyline would be unthinkable without the influences of the Mid-Century Modern Style, which for decades provided the basis for buildings such as the Willis Tower, the Daley Center, the Inland Steel Building, and Chase Tower, to name only a few.

The Bauhaus continues to be deeply and uniquely intertwined with the history of Chicago. Architect Dirk Lohan, Mies' grandson, highlights the innovative, creative, and progressive nature of the school and states that, upon its founding, the Bauhaus "influenced almost all architects and designers in the entire world." Ultimately, the Bauhaus remains true to its cryptic, yet global and promising name: a house in which building is done.

ein, versah seine Bauten mit Vorhangfassaden und entwickelte den Begriff des „Universalraums": ein großer, unverbauter Raum in einem Gebäude, der den Bewohnern zur individuellen Gestaltung offensteht.

DIE SKYLINE VON CHICAGO WÄRE OHNE DIE EINFLÜSSE DES MID-CENTURY MODERN STYLE NICHT VORSTELLBAR.

Der International Style, heute auch Mid-Century Modern Style genannt, zu dessen Begründern Mies van der Rohe gemeinsam mit Gropius und Le Corbusier zu zählen ist, gab eine industrielle und unpersönliche Gestaltung vor, die in Verbindung mit ihrer internationalen Ausrichtung bald weltweit Anklang fand. Die ästhetischen Elemente der modernen Architektur, einschließlich der Abkehr von der traditionellen Ornamentik, die Verwendung rasterartiger Muster und die Integration modularer statt symmetrischer Einheiten nahmen immensen Einfluss auf die architektonische Entwicklung in den USA. Das Ergebnis war ein ehrlicher, offener Ansatz, der die Gebäudekonstruktion, beispielsweise das Stahlskelett, sichtbar macht und durch Materialien wie Stahl, Glas, Beton oder Granit geprägt ist. Die Skyline von Chicago wäre ohne die Einflüsse des Mid-Century Modern Style nicht vorstellbar, der jahrzehntelang die Grundlage für Bauten wie den Willis Tower, das Daley Center, das Inland Steel Building und den Chase Tower bildete, um nur einige zu nennen.

Bis heute ist die Geschichte des Bauhauses auf enge und besondere Weise mit der Geschichte Chicagos verbunden. Architekt Dirk Lohan, ein Enkel von Mies van der Rohe, unterstreicht den innovativen, kreativen und progressiven Charakter der Schule und erklärt, dass das Bauhaus nach seiner Gründung „fast alle Architekten und Designer auf der ganzen Welt beeinflusst hat".

Am Ende bleibt das Bauhaus seinem kryptischen, aber globalen und vielversprechenden Namen treu: Ein Haus, das im Bau ist, und ein Haus, in dem gebaut wird.

BAUHAUS DANCES – MOVEMENT AT THE BAUHAUS

Franz Anton Cramer

The Bauhaus is known above all for its achievements in the field of architecture, the fine arts and design. The role of dance and movement in the training courses of the Bauhaus is often neglected.[1] *This is because it was first and foremost a university, but the new teaching concepts that were first tried out in Weimar and later in Dessau also relied on the stage, more precisely the dance stage and set design in a broader sense.*

HE WAS INTERESTED IN EXPLORING THE BASIC RULES OF COMPOSITION, THE ANIMATION OF SPACE AND THE POSITION OF THE HUMAN OR THE HUMAN BODY IN THE SPATIAL STRUCTURE.

Oskar Schlemmer had been working on his major project Triadisches Ballett *(Triadic Ballet) since before World War I. Bauhaus protagonists were also present at the premiere in Stuttgart in 1922. They were so impressed by what they saw that they immediately engaged Schlemmer as a teacher. On his arrival in Weimar, Schlemmer first tackled the installation of the so-called Bauhaus Stage. It was part of his educational concept in painting classes. He was interested in exploring the basic rules of composition, the animation of space and the position of the human or the human body in the spatial structure. What could be more natural than to make the pictorial space of the stage a subject of study in painting and sculptural design?*

After moving into the specially built new Bauhaus building in Dessau, Schlemmer then had a – as we would say today – multifunctional space available for his research: The large auditorium and cafeteria, the connecting element of the various

BAUHAUSTÄNZE – BEWEGUNG AM BAUHAUS

Franz Anton Cramer

Das Bauhaus ist vor allem bekannt für seine Leistungen im Bereich der Architektur, der bildenden Kunst und des Designs – oder der Gestaltung, wie man damals sagte.[1] *Unbeleuchtet bleibt meist die Rolle des Tanzes und der Bewegung in den Ausbildungsgängen des Bauhauses. Denn dieses war ja zuallererst eine Hochschule, und die neuen Lehrkonzepte, die zuerst in Weimar und später in Dessau ausprobiert wurden, stützten sich auch auf die Bühne, genauer gesagt die Tanzbühne und im erweiterten Sinne das Bühnenbild.*

ER INTERESSIERTE SICH FÜR DIE ERFORSCHUNG VON GRUNDREGELN DER KOMPOSITION, FÜR DIE BELEBUNG DES RAUMS UND FÜR DIE STELLUNG DES MENSCHEN BEZIEHUNGSWEISE SEINES KÖRPERS IM RAUMGEFÜGE.

Oskar Schlemmer hatte schon seit der Zeit vor dem Ersten Weltkrieg an seinem großen Projekt Triadisches Ballett *gearbeitet. Bei der Uraufführung 1922 in Stuttgart waren auch die führenden Vertreter des Bauhauses anwesend. Sie zeigten sich vom Gesehenen so beeindruckt, dass sie Schlemmer sogleich als Lehrkraft verpflichteten. In Weimar angekommen, sorgte Schlemmer als Erstes für die Einrichtung der sogenannten Bauhausbühne. Sie war Teil seines pädagogischen Konzepts im Fach Malerei. Er interessierte sich für die Erforschung von Grundregeln der Komposition, für die Belebung des Raums und für die Stellung des Menschen beziehungsweise seines Körpers im Raumgefüge. Was lag näher, als den Bildraum der Bühne zum Studienobjekt der Malerei und der plastischen Gestaltung zu machen?*

building wings (workshops, studios, lobby and residential wing), could be converted into a stage with sliding walls. This is where the performances took place; the sets and costumes were manufactured in the studios.

HERE, DANCE WAS A KIND OF SECONDARY DISCIPLINE IN THE SERVICE OF THE VISUAL ARTS.

Schlemmer was well acquainted with the milieu of new modernist dance. But in contrast to the individual artistic or community-based pursuit of expressive dance such as that of Mary Wigman or Rudolf von Laban, Schlemmer's research laboratory for dance dealt with the exploration of pictorial laws that regulate the body in space, its changeability and its plastic possibilities. Here, dance was a kind of secondary discipline in the service of the visual arts. The alienation of the human figure through attached objects such as in the Stäbetanz (pole or stick dance), the emphasis on the flow of movement in the Reifentanz (hoops dance) or the shift to materiality in the Metalltanz (metal dance) or Glastanz (glass dance) are still inspirational for dance today, as seen in the 2002 production Formas Breves by the Brazilian choreographer Lia Rodrigues or in Raphael Hillebrand's POW 2045 of 2014. Several reconstruction projects, in particular that of Gerhard Bohner in 1980, have repeatedly brought Schlemmer's research back into the present.

Although Oskar Schlemmer was one of the most important stage artists of the 1920s, he was not a true "theater man." The large numbers of scenic works that he realized with his students for the Bauhaus Stage were not intended as theatrical works of art in the narrower sense, but rather as a spatialization of pictorial compositional strategies. In any case, the diverse studies by the modernists of a theater that is abstracted from humanity were located at the interface of performing and visual arts. Das mechanische Ballett (1923) by Kurt Schmidt and Wassily Kandinsky's Bilder einer Ausstellung (1928) were also created at the Bauhaus and completely dispense with the depiction of human bodies.[2] The avant-garde phantasm of a theater stage of forms, colors and light, populated entire-

Nach dem Umzug in das eigens errichtete neue Bauhausgebäude in Dessau stand Schlemmer dann ein – wie wir heute sagen würden – Multifunktionsraum für seine Forschungen zur Verfügung: Die große Aula und zugleich Mensa, verbindendes Element der verschiedenen Gebäudeflügel (Werkstätten, Ateliers, Foyer und Wohntrakt) konnte mit Gleitwänden zur Bühne umfunktioniert werden. Dort fanden die Aufführungen statt.

TANZ WAR HIER EINE ART SEKUNDÄRDISZIPLIN IM DIENST DER BILDENDEN KUNST.

Schlemmer kannte sich recht gut aus im Milieu des neuen Tanzes der Moderne. Aber im Gegensatz zum individualkünstlerischen oder gemeinschaftsstiftenden Streben des Ausdruckstanzes etwa einer Mary Wigman oder eines Rudolf von Laban befasste sich Schlemmers Forschungslabor für Tanz mit der Ergründung bildnerischer Gesetze, die den Körper im Raum, seine Veränderbarkeit und seine plastischen Möglichkeiten regeln. Tanz war hier eine Art Sekundärdisziplin im Dienst der bildenden Kunst. Die Verfremdungen der menschlichen Gestalt durch angefügte Objekte, etwa im Stäbetanz, die Betonung des Bewegungsflusses im Reifentanz oder die Hinwendung zur Materialität von Werkstoffen im Metalltanz oder Glastanz sind bis heute Inspiration für tänzerisches Schaffen, so zu sehen in der Produktion Formas Breves der brasilianischen Choreografin Lia Rodrigues 2002 oder in Raphael Hillebrands POW 2045 aus dem Jahr 2014. Mehrere Rekonstruktionsprojekte, insbesondere das von Gerhard Bohner aus dem Jahr 1980, haben Schlemmers Forschungen immer wieder in die Gegenwart geholt.

Oskar Schlemmer zählt zwar zu den bedeutenden Bühnenkünstlern der 1920er-Jahre; ein echter „Theatermann" war er jedoch nicht. Die szenischen Arbeiten im Rahmen der Bauhausbühne, die er mit seinen Studenten in großer Zahl realisierte, waren nicht im engeren Sinne als Theaterkunstwerke gedacht, sondern als Verräumlichung bildkompositorischer Strategien. Ohnehin waren die vielfältigen Recherchen der Moderne zu einem Theater, das vom Menschen abstrahiert, eher

ly by puppets and marionettes, was also explored in experimental works by Erika Giovanna Klien in the context of Viennese kinetics, for instance in the 1926 Kinetic Marionette Theater,[3] or by the Russian mathematician and author Julia Sazonova.[4] And the French-influenced dance avant-garde undertook similar experiments with the productions Parade (1917, Ballets Russes) and Relâche (1924, Ballets suédois).

We can assume that Schlemmer was familiar with the debates of his time: In the program booklet written for the premiere of the Triadisches Ballett in 1922, he refers directly to the Ballets Russes and the Ballets suédois,[5] which adhered much more to overall theatrical effect, but by involving well-known painters and sculptors of their time aimed at pictorial effects while evoking other forms of representation of the human body through costumes and the use of masks.[6] Schlemmer's participation in the important International Exhibition of New Theater Techniques in Vienna in 1924 also tied his own work into that of the international avant-garde.

THE BAUHAUS AND ABOVE ALL THE BAUHAUS STAGE UNDER OSKAR SCHLEMMER EXERTED A HITHERTO COMPLETELY UNDERESTIMATED INFLUENCE ON THE EVOLUTION OF DANCE.

In the program booklet for the Stuttgart premiere, Schlemmer wrote a manifesto-like essay entitled "Ballet? Reflections on the current situation of stage dance." He turns against "the flutteriness of today's dancers of the dance" and contrasts it with his own work, "which flirts with the cheerful without forfeiting the grotesque" and "ultimately strives to dematerialize the body." Thus, he builds on the tendency of his time and considers whether the Triadisches Ballett does not "show the beginnings of what might develop into a German ballet." This question is no longer asked today. But Schlemmer's educational concept is significant for modernist dance because he was interested in artistic experimentation and researching visual movement as emancipation from the figurative. The Bauhaus and above all the Bauhaus Stage under Oskar Schlemmer

im Grenzbereich zwischen darstellender und bildender Kunst angesiedelt. Das Mechanische Ballett (1923) von Kurt Schmidt oder Wassily Kandinskys Bilder einer Ausstellung (1928) waren ebenfalls am Bauhaus entstanden und verzichteten völlig auf die Darstellung menschlicher Körper.[2] Das avantgardistische Phantasma einer rein durch Puppen und Marionetten bevölkerten Theaterbühne der Formen, der Farben und des Lichts wurde auch in experimentellen Arbeiten von Erika Giovanna Klien im Umfeld des Wiener Kinetismus untersucht, so etwa mit dem Kinetischen Marionettentheater 1926,[3] oder von der russischen Mathematikerin und Literatin Julia Sazonova[4]. Und auch die französisch geprägte Tanzavantgarde unternahm mit den Produktionen Parade (1917, Ballets russes) oder Relâche (1924, Ballets suédois) vergleichbare Experimente.

Dass Schlemmer sich in den Debatten seiner Zeit auskannte, darf vorausgesetzt werden: Im Programmheft der Uraufführung zum Triadischen Ballett 1922 bezieht er sich direkt auf die Ballets russes und die Ballets suédois,[5] die zwar weit mehr am theatralischen Gesamteffekt festhielten, jedoch durch Hinzuziehung namhafter Maler und Bildhauer ihrer Zeit auf Bildwirkungen abzielten, andererseits durch Kostümierungen und den Gebrauch von Masken andere Repräsentationsformen des menschlichen Körpers evozierten.[6] Auch Schlemmers Teilnahme an der bedeutenden Internationalen Ausstellung neuer Theatertechnik 1924 in Wien band sein eigenes Schaffen in das der internationalen Avantgarde ein.

DAS BAUHAUS UND VOR ALLEM AUCH DIE BAUHAUSBÜHNE UNTER OSKAR SCHLEMMER ÜBTEN EINEN BISLANG VÖLLIG UNTERSCHÄTZTEN EINFLUSS AUF DIE ENTWICKLUNG DES TANZES AUS.

Im Programmheft zur Stuttgarter Uraufführung entwickelte Schlemmer in einem manifestartigen Textbeitrag mit dem Titel Ballett? Überlegungen zur aktuellen Lage des Bühnentanzes. Er wendet sich gegen „die Flatterseligkeit heutiger Tänzetänzerinnen" und stellt dagegen sein eigenes Werk, „das mit dem Heiteren kokettiert, ohne der Groteske zu verfallen" und „zuletzt Entmateriali-

exerted a hitherto completely underestimated influence on the evolution of dance.[7]

1 Literature: To this day, the fundamental and authoritative book on Oskar Schlemmer's theater work is that by Dirk Scheper (whose parents worked at the Bauhaus Dessau): Scheper, Dirk, Oskar Schlemmer. Das Triadische Ballett und die Bauhausbühne, (Berlin, 1988). The facts and dates in this article are based on the research and information published there as well as on the archival materials cited.

2 A new version of Kandinsky's work was produced in January 2019 as part of the event series 100 Years of Bauhaus – The Opening Festival by the Akademie der Künste Berlin. The Theater der Klänge in Düsseldorf has also worked for many years on reinterpretations of the Bauhaus repertoire.

3 See Bast, Gerald et al., (eds.), Wiener Kinetismus. Eine bewegte Moderne / Viennese kineticism. Modernism in motion, exh. cat. Dynamik! Kubismus, Futurismus, Kinetismus, Unteres Belvedere, Vienna, (Vienna/New York, 2011).

4 See the detailed monograph by Keith Tribble, The Puppet Theatres of Julia Sazonova-Slonimskaia, Puppetry Yearbook no. 6, (Lewiston/New York, 2004).

5 Both were legendary theatrical undertakings of early modernism. From 1909 to 1929, the Ballets Russes impressed the world with its innovations on classical dance, especially with The Afternoon of a Faun (1912) and The Rite of Spring (1913). Although the Ballets suédois (1920–1925) was shorter-lived, it was even more radical in its interdisciplinary aesthetics and ultimately even integrated film and literature into its performances.

6 A much-discussed example of this is the Ballets suédois's La Création du monde of 1923, in which the dancers disappeared inside full-body costumes and behind oversized masks. Gerhard Bohner choreographed a new version of it in 1974, and Faustin Linyekula in 2013.

7 Sigrid Pawelke examined this dimension in her study of the continuation of Bauhaus teachings in the United States. See Sigrid Pawelke, Einflüsse der Bauhausbühne in den USA. Eine Untersuchung zur Verbindung von Bauhausbühne und amerikanischer Bühnenperformance und Postmodern Dance unter ästhetischen und pädagogischen Aspekten, (Regensburg, 2005).

sierung der Körper erstrebt". Damit knüpft er an die Tendenz seiner Zeit an und visioniert, ob das Triadische Ballett nicht „die Anfänge zeigt, daraus sich ein deutsches Ballett entwickeln könnte". Diese Frage stellt sich heute nicht mehr. Doch ist Schlemmers pädagogische Konzeption bedeutsam für den Tanz der Moderne, denn es ging ihm um künstlerisches Experiment und visuelle Bewegungsforschung im Zeichen der Emanzipation vom Figurativen. Das Bauhaus und vor allem auch die Bauhausbühne unter Oskar Schlemmer übten einen bislang völlig unterschätzten Einfluss auf die Entwicklung des Tanzes aus.[7]

1 Literatur: Das bis heute grundlegende Werk zur Theaterarbeit Oskar Schlemmers stammt von Dirk Scheper (dessen Eltern am Bauhaus Dessau tätig waren): Dirk Scheper, Oskar Schlemmer. Das Triadische Ballett und die Bauhausbühne, Berlin 1988. Vorliegender Beitrag stützt sich in Sach- und Zeitangaben auf die hier publizierten Forschungen und Angaben, teilweise auch auf die zitierten Archivalien.

2 Eine Neufassung von Kandinskys Werk erfolgte im Januar 2019 im Rahmen der Veranstaltungsreihe 100 Jahre Bauhaus – Das Eröffnungsfestival der Akademie der Künste Berlin. Auch das Theater der Klänge in Düsseldorf befasst sich seit vielen Jahren mit Neuinterpretationen des Bauhausrepertoires.

3 Vgl. Wiener Kinetismus. Eine bewegte Moderne. / Viennese kineticism. Modernism in motion, hrsg. von Gerald Bast u. a., Katalog zur Ausstellung Dynamik! Kubismus, Futurismus, Kinetismus, Wien, Unteres Belvedere, Wien, Wien/New York 2011.

4 Vgl. die ausführliche monografische Darstellung von Keith Tribble, The Puppet Theatres of Julia Sazonova-Slonimskaia, Lewiston/New York 2004 (= Puppetry Yearbook, 6).

5 Beides waren legendäre Theaterunternehmungen der frühen Moderne. Die Ballets russes beeindruckten von 1909 bis 1929 die Welt mit ihren Innovationen der klassischen Tanzschule, insbesondere mit Nachmittag eines Fauns (1912) und Das Frühlingsopfer (1913). Die Ballets suédois (1920–1925) waren zwar kurzlebiger, dafür aber noch radikaler in ihrer interdisziplinären Ästhetik und integrierten zuletzt sogar Film und Literatur in ihre Aufführungen.

6 Viel diskutiertes Beispiel hierfür ist La Création du monde der Ballets suédois von 1923, bei dem die Tänzer in Ganzkörperkostümen und hinter überdimensionalen Masken verschwanden. Gerhard Bohner choreografierte 1974 eine Neufassung, Faustin Linyekula 2013.

7 Diese Dimension untersuchte Sigrid Pawelke in ihrer Studie über das Fortleben der Bauhauspädagogik in den Vereinigten Staaten, vgl. Sigrid Pawelke, Einflüsse der Bauhausbühne in den USA. Eine Untersuchung zur Verbindung von Bauhausbühne und amerikanischer Bühnenperformance und Postmodern Dance unter ästhetischen und pädagogischen Aspekten, Regensburg 2005.

GOETHE, BAUHAUS AND LIGHT

Kristina Lowis

From 2016 to 2018, in the exhibition series A Little Piece of Bauhaus, *the Goethe-Institut Chicago presented works and work processes by eight artists from Germany and the United States exploring the traces of the Bauhaus in Chicago. Two anniversaries provided the official occasion: 2017 marked the 80th anniversary of the founding of the New Bauhaus and later Institute of Design (ID), and 2019 marks* 100 Years of Bauhaus. *No one knew then how appropriate the period would turn out to be for this transatlantic exploration of the history and impact of a school. From the larger whole, "a little piece of Bauhaus" suffices as a starting and reference point for independent work, encounters with creative approaches and identifying personal positions.*

HE HAD AN "INSTITUTE OF LIGHT" IN MIND THAT WOULD STUDY AND UNDERSTAND LIGHT AS A MATERIAL IN ITSELF.

The Bauhaus was an established constant as an avant-garde school, a position and a "brand." Many alumni of the academy, which closed in Berlin in 1933, continued their work in exile in the USA, but only Chicago's New Bauhaus referenced it in its name. Its artistically polyvalent director, the former Bauhaus teacher, freelancer and immigrant László Moholy-Nagy, had big plans. He had an "Institute of Light" in mind that would study and understand light as a material in itself. Consequently, he named one of the six workshops at the new school, a place that would work with light, the Light Workshop. Photography was located here. The versatility of the medium conceived is illustrated by the pointed yet poetic definition by Arthur Siegel, who decisively

GOETHE, BAUHAUS UND DAS LICHT

Kristina Lowis

Von 2016 bis 2018 zeigte das Goethe-Institut Chicago in der Ausstellungsreihe A Little Piece of Bauhaus *Arbeiten und Werkprozesse von neun Künstler*innen aus Deutschland und den USA, die in Chicago auf Bauhausspuren wandelten. Den offiziellen Anlass boten zwei Jubiläen: 2017 jährte sich zum 80. Mal die Gründung des New Bauhaus und späteren Institute of Design (ID), 2019 sind es* 100 Jahre Bauhaus. *Nicht vorhersehbar war, als wie passend sich der Zeitraum für diese transatlantische Auseinandersetzung mit der Geschichte und Wirkung einer Schule erweisen sollte. „Ein Stück Bauhaus" aus dem großen Ganzen genügt als Ausgangs- und Bezugspunkt für freies Arbeiten, die Begegnung mit gestalterischen Ansätzen und eigene Positionsbestimmung.*

IHM SCHWEBTE EIN „INSTITUTE OF LIGHT", EIN INSTITUT FÜR LICHTFORSCHUNG, VOR. LICHT SOLLTE ALS EIGENSTÄNDIGES MATERIAL BEGRIFFEN WERDEN.

Das Bauhaus war als Avantgardeschule, als Haltung und „Marke" eine feste Größe. Zahlreiche Ehemalige der 1933 in Berlin geschlossenen Hochschule setzten ihre Arbeit im Exil in den USA fort, doch nur das Chicagoer New Bauhaus führte die Referenz im Namen. Sein künstlerisch polyvalenter Direktor – der einstige Bauhauslehrer, Freiberufler und Immigrant László Moholy-Nagy – führte Großes im Schilde. Ihm schwebte ein „Institute of Light", ein Institut für Lichtforschung, vor. Licht sollte als eigenständiges Material begriffen werden. Folgerichtig nannte er eine der sechs Werkstätten an der neuen Schule „Light Workshop", Lichtwerkstatt: ein Ort, an dem mit Licht als Werkstoff gearbeitet wurde. Hier war die Fotografie angesiedelt. Wie vielseitig

shaped the photography program at the ID. He wrote, “Photography is [...] science, system, process, technique, tool, documentation, pages from life, creative treatment of actuality, archives of memory, mirrors of memory, extension of the eye, enlargement of vision, hobby, business, profession, means of expression, way of life, poor man’s Rorschach, language, art, etc., etc., etc.”[1] His colleague, the famous photographer Harry Callahan, advised students to just start taking pictures in the first semester to find out who they really were, and then to use them for a project in the second semester. Imitation was frowned upon; it was important for each student to find their own questions. Thus a space was created in Chicago in which trying things out became the method, experimentation a system. This is, perhaps, the most important thing that the new Bauhaus borrowed from the old.

THUS A SPACE WAS CREATED IN CHICAGO IN WHICH TRYING THINGS OUT BECAME THE METHOD, EXPERIMENTATION A SYSTEM.

The fact that photography has lost nothing of its capacity to assist thought processes and that light continues to be a popular material is demonstrated by the fact that most of the artists now invited by the Goethe-Institut Chicago approach their subject with photography. Ludwig Mies van der Rohe’s architecture is central to this. In a free further progression of Mies’ architectural collages, Assaf Evron’s photographs offer alternative views of the historical buildings and their components by means of mirror images and skillful, abstracting detail images. In 2014, Doug Fogelson documented the ID’s former darkroom in the basement of the Crown Hall on the campus of the Illinois Institute of Technology (IIT) shortly before its demolition. At the same time, he used analogue photograms – from architectural models discarded by the IIT, vinyl singles of the 1950s and film strips and audio tapes – to take up the transience of formal designs and storage media as well as to explore what ought to be saved over time and what left behind.

Mies’ Lafayette Park in 1960s Detroit was the topic for Rebecca Wilton, who, like Christina

das Medium aufgefasst wurde, verdeutlicht die poetisch-pointierte Definition Arthur Siegels, der das Fotoprogramm am ID maßgeblich prägte: „Fotografie ist [...] Wissenschaft, System, Prozess, Technik, Werkzeug, Dokumentation, Seiten des Lebens, kreatives Umgehen mit dem Tagesgeschehen, Archive der Erinnerung, Spiegel der Erinnerung, Erweiterung des Auges, erweitertes Sehen, Hobby, Geschäft, Beruf, usdrucksmittel, Lebensart, Rorschach für Arme, Sprache, Kunst usw. usw., usw.“ Sein Kollege, der berühmte Fotograf Harry Callahan, riet dazu, im ersten Semester einfach drauflos zu fotografieren, um herauszufinden, wer man eigentlich ist, um dann im zweiten Semester daraus ein Projekt zu machen. Nachahmen war verpönt, es kam darauf an, eigene Fragestellungen zu finden. So entstand in Chicago ein Raum, in dem das Ausprobieren zur Methode, das Experiment zum System wurde. Vielleicht liegt hier die wichtigste Übernahme des neuen aus dem alten Bauhaus.

SO ENTSTAND IN CHICAGO EIN RAUM, IN DEM DAS AUSPROBIEREN ZUR METHODE, DAS EXPERIMENT ZUM SYSTEM WURDE.

Dass die Fotografie nichts von ihrer Kapazität als dem Gehirn vorgelagerte Denkhilfe eingebüßt hat und Licht als Werkstoff weiter gut im Kurs steht, zeigt sich in der Tatsache, dass die Mehrzahl der nun vom Goethe-Institut Chicago eingeladenen Künstler*innen sich ihrem Gegenstand mit Lichtbildern nähert. Ludwig Mies van der Rohes Architektur ist dabei zentral. So bietet Assaf Evron in einer freien Weiterentwicklung von Mies’ Architekturcollagen in seinen Fotografien alternative Sichtweisen der historischen Bauten und ihrer Bestandteile, durch Spiegelungen und geschickte, abstrahierende Teilaufnahmen. Doug Fogelson dokumentierte 2014 die kurz vor dem Abriss stehende ehemalige Dunkelkammer des ID in der Crown Hall auf dem Campus des Illinois Institute of Technology (IIT). Parallel thematisierte er mit analogen Fotogrammen – von am IIT entsorgten Architekturmodellen, Vinylsingles der 1950er-Jahre sowie Film- und Tonbandstreifen – die Vergänglichkeit von Formentwürfen und Speichermedien, aber auch, was durch die Zeit zu retten, was mit der Zeit zurückzulassen ist.

Wildgrube, uses photography to query the history, condition and atmosphere of historical complexes and to visually capture her own viewpoint. While Wilton produces impressive, tranquil views, Wildgrube approaches Walter Gropius' Dessau-Törten housing estate of the 1920s with varied, sometimes seemingly incidental views. When the artist duo Luftwerk, in turn, projects its very own vision of Mies' Farnsworth House onto the building, it provides explanations, creation and interpretation all at once with these unexpected views. Josef Albers, who moved from the Bauhaus to Black Mountain College in North Carolina, is the inspiration for the Chicago painter Serene Wise, who examines her perception in the light gradations of the color gray. Monika Wulfers, who moved from Berlin to Chicago, updated Oskar Schlemmer's ballets with her angular neon compositions. Her installations structurally rearrange spaces, whereas Heike Albrecht's dance experiments transfer Schlemmer's approach to the present time and illustrate perspectives of the relationship between humans, movement and space.

SPACES FOR FREEDOM TO THINK AND LEARN, FOR EXPERIMENTING AND TURNING TO THE OUTSIDE WORLD, FOR ILLUMINATING ONE'S OWN AND OTHERS' POSITIONS – AND FOR OUR COMMON HOPE THAT THE LIGHT WILL NOT GO OUT ON US.

The overarching question of the Bauhaus anniversary is: How do works and ideas from this school relate to us today? What can this cultural heritage stand for? In the winter of 2016–2017, while on a curator research trip for the Goethe-Institut in preparation for the exhibition New Bauhaus Chicago: Experiment Photography and Film for the Bauhaus-Archiv / Museum für Gestaltung in Berlin, my own encounters with contemporary photographers in Chicago unexpectedly led to an open political exchange. Since many of the shadows cast by the presidential election at that time have caught up with us and – along with many other worsened situations – mean cuts in education, intellectual life and funding for the arts, in my view "Goethe"

Mies' Lafayette Park in Detroit aus den 1960er-Jahren war Thema für Rebecca Wilton, die wie Christina Wildgrube Fotografie dazu benutzt, Geschichte, Zustand und Atmosphäre historischer Anlagen zu befragen und ihre eigene Sicht bildlich zu fassen. Während Wilton eindrucksvolle, stille Ansichten erzeugt, tastet sich Wildgrube mit vielgestaltigen, zum Teil wie beiläufigen Ansichten an Walter Gropius' Siedlung Dessau-Törten aus den 1920er-Jahren heran. Wenn das Künstlerduo Luftwerk wiederum seine ganz eigene Vision von Mies' Farnsworth House auf den Bau projiziert, liefert es mit diesen ungeahnten Anblicken Erläuterung, Kreation und Interpretation zugleich. Josef Albers, vom Bauhaus ans Black Mountain College in North Carolina gewechselt, steht Pate für die Inspiration der Chicagoer Malerin Serene Wise, die in den Lichtstufen der Farbe Grau ihre Wahrnehmung überprüft. Monika Wulfers, von Berlin nach Chicago übergesiedelt, aktualisiert mit ihren Neongeraden-Kompositionen Oskar Schlemmers Ballette. Ihre Installationen legen Räume statisch neu aus, Heike Albrechts Tanzexperimente dagegen übertragen Schlemmers Herangehen bewegt in die Jetztzeit und zeigen Perspektiven des Verhältnisses zwischen Mensch, Bewegung und Raum auf.

RÄUME ZUM FREIEN DENKEN UND LERNEN, EXPERIMENTIEREN UND HINWENDEN ZUR AUSSENWELT, ZUM AUSLEUCHTEN EIGENER UND FREMDER HALTUNGEN – UND FÜR DIE GEMEINSAME HOFFNUNG, DASS (UNS) DAS LICHT NICHT AUSGEHT.

Die übergreifende Frage des Bauhausjubiläums lautet: Welchen Bezug finden wir heute zu Werken und Ideen aus dieser Schule? Wofür kann ein solches Kulturerbe stehen? Meine eigenen Begegnungen mit zeitgenössischen Fotograf*innen in Chicago, auf einer Kuratoren-Rechercheresie des Goethe-Instituts in Vorbereitung der Ausstellung New Bauhaus Chicago: Experiment Fotografie und Film für das Bauhaus-Archiv / Museum für Gestaltung in Berlin, gerieten im Winter 2016/17 unverhofft zu einem offenen politischen Austausch. Da etliche der damals durch die US-Präsidentenwahl vorausgeworfenen Schatten uns

and "Bauhaus" should currently, above all, open up spaces. Spaces for freedom to think and learn, for experimenting and turning to the outside world, for illuminating one's own and others' positions – and for our common hope that the light will not go out on us.

1 *Arthur Siegel, "Photography is," in: "Five Photography Students from the Institute of Design, Illinois Institute of Technology," special issue,* Aperture 9, 2 *(1961), p. 3.*

inzwischen eingeholt haben und – neben vielen anderen Schlechterstellungen – Einschnitte in Bildung, Geistesleben und Kunstförderung bedeuten, sollten „Goethe" und „Bauhaus" aus meiner Sicht gegenwärtig vor allem Räume aufspannen: zum freien Denken und Lernen, Experimentieren und Hinwenden zur Außenwelt, zum Ausleuchten eigener und fremder Haltungen – und für die gemeinsame Hoffnung, dass (uns) das Licht nicht ausgeht.

1 *Arthur Siegel, „Photography is", in:* Five Photography Students from the Institute of Design, *hrsg. von Illinois Institute of Technology, Rochester 1961 (=Aperture-Sonderheft), [S. 3].*

BIOGRAPHIES
BIOGRAFIEN

Heike Albrecht

After her career in education, Heike Albrecht studied Dance and Performing Arts at the Moving On Center – School for Participatory Arts and Research in Oakland, CA, USA. She focuses in her work on intentions and interactions that translate the human body and keep it in a translatable state. She directed the Performing Arts Program at the LOFFT in Leipzig, the interdisciplinary festival WESTEND 04/05 Leipzig, and the Biennale Tanznacht Berlin. From 2007 to 2010 she was artistic director and managing director of the Berlin Sophiensaele. She was program director/dramaturge for the theatre festival FAVORITEN 2012 in North Rhine-Westphalia and curated the format "As we speak" for the Goethe-Institut as part of the European Capital of Culture "Maribor 2012." In 2018–19 she worked as a curator and research assistant at the Akademie der Künste in Berlin.

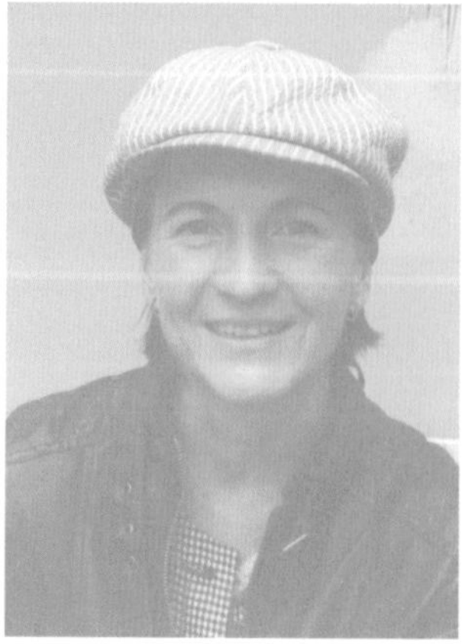

Heike Albrecht

Heike Albrecht studierte nach ihrer pädagogischen Laufbahn Tanz und Performing Arts am Moving On Center – School for Participatory Arts and Research in Oakland, CA. Im Zentrum ihrer Arbeit stehen Interaktionen, die die Konkretheit des Körpers übersetzen respektive übersetzbar halten. Sie leitete das Performing Arts Programm am LOFFT, das interdisziplinäre Festival WESTEND 04/05 in Leipzig sowie die Biennale Tanznacht Berlin 2006 und 2014. 2007–2010 war sie Künstlerische Leiterin und Geschäftsführerin der Berliner Sophiensaele. Für das Theaterfestival FAVORITEN 2012 in Nordrhein-Westfalen war sie Programmleiterin/Dramaturgin und kuratierte für das Goethe-Institut das Format As we speak *im Rahmen der Europäischen Kulturhauptstadt Maribor 2012. Darüber hinaus arbeitet sie als Dramaturgin, somatische Bewegungstrainerin und Jurorin. 2018/19 ist sie künstlerisch-wissenschaftliche Mitarbeiterin und Kuratorin an der Akademie der Künste in Berlin.*

Franz Anton Cramer

Franz Anton Cramer is a dance scholar and an author. Since 2003 he has been researching archival processes of the performing arts with a focus on dance. He works as a lecturer at art academies and universities, most recently at the HZT Berlin and at the University of Salzburg. From 2007 until 2013 he was a Fellow at the Collège international de philosophie in Paris, and in 2011 a Villa Kamogawa scholarship holder at the Goethe-Institut Kyoto. Together with Barbara Büscher, he has been publishing the e-journal MAP – Media Archive Performance *(www.perfomap.de) since 2009. In 2008 he published the monograph* In aller Freiheit. Tanzkultur in Frankreich zwischen 1930 und 1950 *(Parodos Verlag, Berlin).*

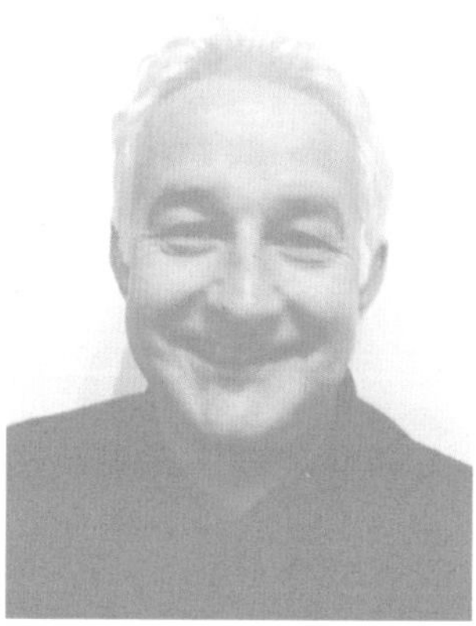

Franz Anton Cramer

Franz Anton Cramer ist Tanzwissenschaftler und Autor. Er forscht seit 2003 über Archivprozesse der Aufführungskünste mit Schwerpunkt Tanz. Er ist an künstlerischen und wissenschaftlichen Hochschulen tätig, zuletzt am HZT Berlin und an der Universität Salzburg. 2007–2013 war er Fellow am Collège international de philosophie in Paris, 2011 Villa Kamogawa-Stipendiat des Goethe-Instituts Kyoto. Gemeinsam mit Barbara Büscher gibt er seit 2009 das E-Journal MAP – Media Archive Performance *(www.perfomap.de) heraus. 2008 erschien von ihm* In aller Freiheit. Tanzkultur in Frankreich zwischen 1930 und 1950 *(Parodos Verlag, Berlin).*

Assaf Evron

Assaf Evron's work investigates the nature of vision and the ways in which it engages with socially constructed edifices, by applying photographic thinking in various two and three-dimensional media. His work has been exhibited in galleries and museums internationally. Evron holds an M.A. from the Cohn Institute as well as an M.F.A. from the School of the Art Institute of Chicago (SAIC), where he currently teaches. He has received numerous awards including a Graham Foundation Exhibition Grant (2017), Israel Lottery, Exhibition Grant (2017) Artis Exhibition Grant (2016), the Israel Museum Jerusalem Gerard Levy Prize for young photographers (2012), the SAIC James Weinstein Fellowship (2012) and the Israeli Ministry of Culture prize for young artists (2010). In the spring of 2019, he will exhibit a special project at the McCormick House in Elmhurst. In fall 2019, he will have his first US museum solo show at the Museum of Contemporary Art Chicago.

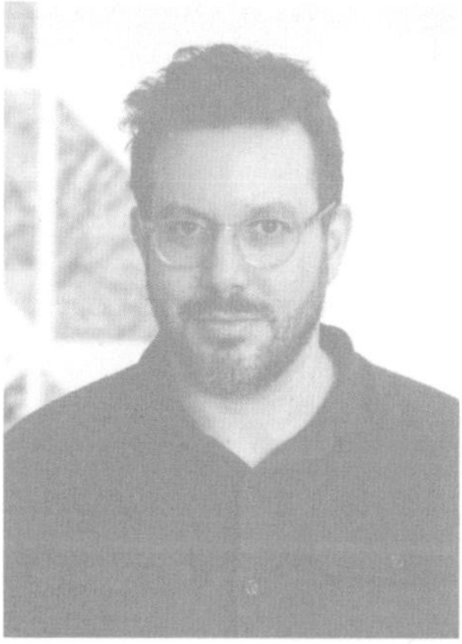

Assaf Evron

Assaf Evron untersucht in seinen Arbeiten das Phänomen des Sehens und wie dieses mit sozial konstruierten Strukturen ineinandergreift, indem er fotografisches Denken in verschiedene zwei- und dreidimensionale Medien einwebt. Seine Arbeiten wurden in Galerien und Museen international ausgestellt. Evron erwarb am Cohn Institute einen M.A. und an der School of the Art Institute of Chicago, an der er heute lehrt, einen M.F.A. Er gewann zahlreiche Auszeichnungen, u.a. den Graham Foundation Exhibition Grant (2017), den Israel Lottery, Exhibition Grant (2017), den Artis Exhibition Grant (2016), den Israel Museum Jerusalem Gerard Levy Preis für junge Fotografen (2012), den SAIC James Weinstein Fellowship (2012) und den Preis für junge Künstler des Israelischen Kulturministeriums (2010). 2019 stellt er im McCormick House in Elmhurst ein Sonderprojekt aus. Im Herbst 2019 zeigt das Museum of Contemporary Art Chicago seine erste Einzelausstellung in den USA.

Doug Fogelson

Doug Fogelson studied at The School of the Art Institute of Chicago and Columbia College Chicago. His artworks have been shown in numerous exhibitions in the US and internationally, including solo shows at the Goethe-Institut Chicago and the Alpineum Produzentengalerie in Lucerne, Switzerland. Group exhibitions including his work have been shown at the Griffin Museum of Photography and the Museum of Contemporary Photography (MoCP) in Chicago. Notable collections holding his work include the MoCP, J. Paul Getty Museum, The Cleveland Clinic, Deloitte and Elmhurst Art Museum among others. Currently, his work is included in the touring exhibition, Bauhaus and Photography. *Doug Fogelson lives and works in Chicago.*

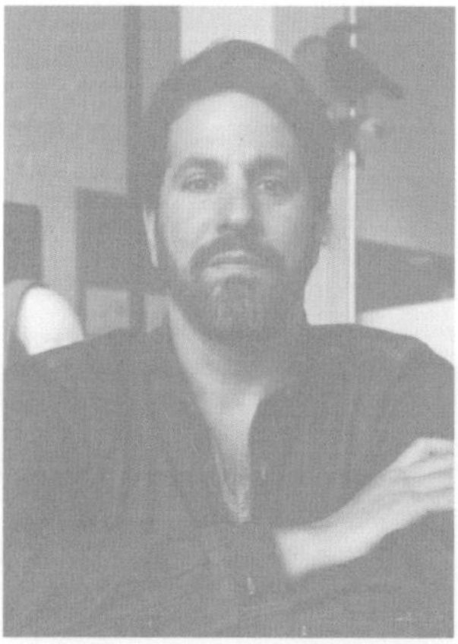

Doug Fogelson

Doug Fogelson studierte an der School of the Art Institute of Chicago und dem Columbia College Chicago. Seine Werke wurden in zahlreichen Ausstellungen in den USA und international gezeigt, darunter Einzelausstellungen am Goethe-Institut Chicago und in der Alpineum Produzentengalerie in Luzern. Gruppenausstellungen mit seinen Arbeiten wurden im Griffin Museum of Photography und im Museum of Contemporary Photography (MoCP) in Chicago gezeigt. Zu den Sammlungen, die seine Werke beherbergen, gehören unter anderem das MoCP, das J. Paul Getty Museum, die Cleveland Clinic, Deloitte und das Elmhurst Art Museum. Zur Zeit ist seine Arbeit in der Wanderausstellung Bauhaus und die Fotografie *zu sehen. Doug Fogelson lebt und arbeitet in Chicago.*

Anke Loh

Anke Loh works as a practicing fashion designer, Chair Emeritus and Associate Professor of the Fashion Department at the School of the Art Institute of Chicago, where she has worked since 2005. Her current research entails finding ways to integrate stretchable circuitry into textiles, ready-to-wear fashion and accessories. She studied Fashion at the Royal Academy of Fine Arts in Antwerp, earning an M.F.A. in 1999, after which she launched her former fashion design company, Rosso NV. Her artistic projects, including Urban Identities, Aloft: Fearless Fashion, and Dressing Light, have attracted international media coverage and recognition, and Loh has been honored as a Laureate at the Festival International des Arts et de la Môde in Hyères, France. Her collections have been featured in international runway shows and showrooms at the New York Fashion Week, Paris' Centre Pompidou, Japan's Osaka Collection Show, and Mode Expo Antwerp, Belgium.

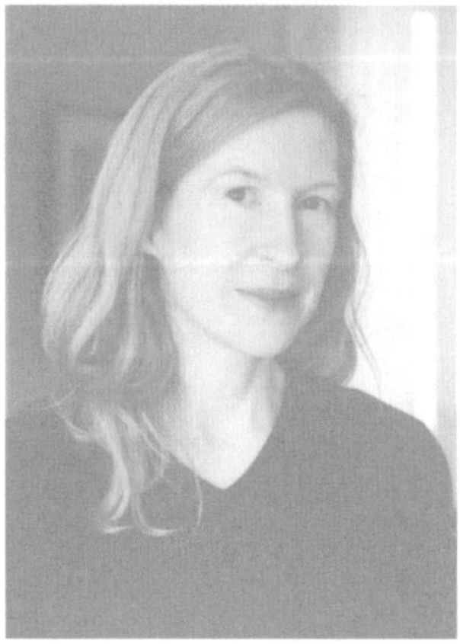

Anke Loh

Anke Loh ist praktizierende Modedesignerin, emeritierte Lehrstuhlinhaberin und außerordentliche Professorin am Fashion Department der School of the Art Institute of Chicago, wo sie seit 2005 tätig ist. Aktuell erforscht sie Verfahren zur Integration dehnbarer Elektronik in Textilien, Konfektionskleidung und Accessoires. Sie absolvierte ein Studium an der Koninklijke Academie voor Schone Kunsten in Antwerpen, das sie 1999 mit dem M.F.A. abschloss. Danach gründete sie ihr ehemaliges Unternehmen für Modedesign, Rosso NV. Ihre Kunstprojekte, darunter Urban Identities, Aloft: Fearless Fashion *und* Dressing Light, *zogen das Interesse und die Anerkennung der internationalen Medien auf sich; unter anderem ist sie Preisträgerin des Festival International des Arts et de la Môde in Hyères (Frankreich). Ihre Kollektionen wurden in internationalen Fashionshows und Showrooms im Rahmen der New York Fashion Week, des Pariser Centre Pompidou, der japanischen Osaka Collection Show und der Mode Expo Antwerp in Belgien gezeigt.*

Kristina Lowis

Kristina Lowis is a freelance curator, author and translator. She completed her Art History studies in 2003 with a dissertation on photographic aesthetics around 1900. She was most recently guest curator of the exhibition New Bauhaus Chicago: Experiment Photography and Film at the Bauhaus-Archiv/Museum für Gestaltung, Berlin. She is currently leading a project indexing the estate of the press photographer Abisag Tüllmann (1935–1996) in the archives of bpk-Bildagentur. Her publications include numerous works on photography from its beginnings to the present, as well as translations from English and French on photography and art from the nineteenth to the twenty-first century.

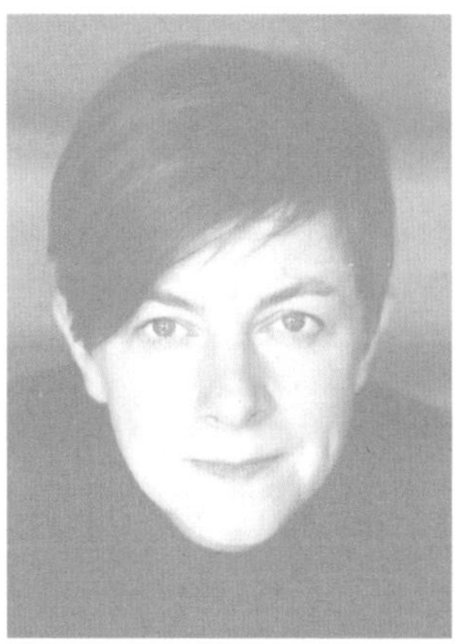

Kristina Lowis

Kristina Lowis ist freie Kuratorin, Autorin und Übersetzerin. Ihr Studium der Kunstgeschichte schloss sie 2003 mit einer Dissertation über Fotografieästhetik um 1900 ab. Sie war zuletzt Gastkuratorin der Ausstellung New Bauhaus Chicago: Experiment Fotografie und Film *im Bauhaus-Archiv/Museum für Gestaltung, Berlin. Aktuell leitet sie ein Projekt zur Nachlasserschließung der Pressefotografin Abisag Tüllmann (1935–1996) im Archiv der bpk-Bildagentur. Zu ihren Publikationen zählen zahlreiche Texte zur Fotografie von ihren Anfängen bis in die Gegenwart sowie Übersetzungen aus dem Englischen und Französischen zu Fotografie und Kunst des 19. bis 21. Jahrhunderts.*

Luftwerk

Petra Bachmaier, originally from Munich, holds an M.A. from the University of Fine Arts Hamburg, Germany. She also holds a B.F.A. from the School of the Art Institute of Chicago and spent an academic semester at the Gerrit Rietveld Academie, Amsterdam.

Sean Gallero, originally from the Bronx, NYC, studied Art and Humanities at Lehman College, with a focus on applied arts and continued studies at the School of the Art Institute of Chicago. Bachmaier and Gallero met during Performance Art studies at SAIC (1999) and have collaborated since 2000.

The artist duo formed Luftwerk in 2007. Luftwerk studio is based in Chicago, IL, USA.

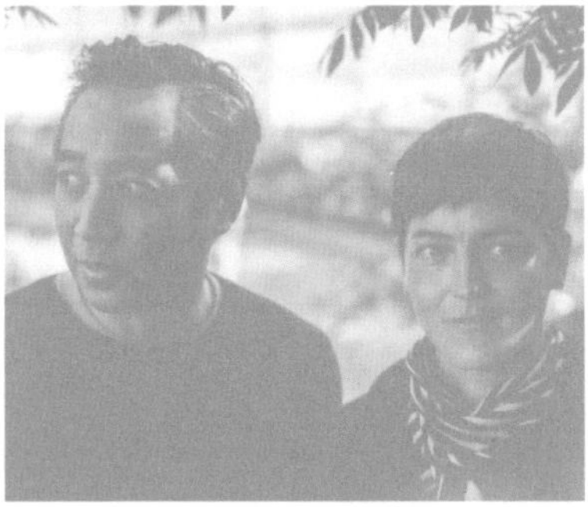

Luftwerk

Petra Bachmaier stammt gebürtig aus München und schloss ihr Studium an der Hochschule für bildende Künste in Hamburg mit dem M.A. ab. Außerdem erwarb sie an der School of the Art Institute of Chicago einen Bachelor of Fine Arts und absolvierte ein Studiensemester an der Gerrit Rietveld Academie in Amsterdam.

Sean Gallero, geboren im New Yorker Stadtteil Bronx, studierte am Lehman College Kunst und Geisteswissenschaften mit dem Schwerpunkt Angewandte Kunst und setzte sein Studium dann an der School of the Art Institute of Chicago fort. Bachmaier und Gallero lernten sich 1999 während ihres Performance Art Studiums an der SAIC kennen und arbeiten seit 2000 zusammen.

Das Künstlerduo gründete im Jahr 2007 das Studio „Luftwerk“ mit Sitz in Chicago, Illinois (USA).

Petra Roggel

Petra Roggel is a graduate economist and a dancer. She worked at the Theater am Halleschen Ufer in Berlin in the 1990s before becoming a freelancer in Berlin's independent scene and working with choreographers such as Xavier Le Roy, Thomas Lehmen and Eszter Salamon. For several years she co-directed the Kaaitheater in Brussels with Johan Reyniers and then joined the Goethe-Institut Head Office in Munich as an expert on dance and performance, where she advised the Goethe-Institutes worldwide. She has been the director of the Goethe-Institut Chicago since 2015.

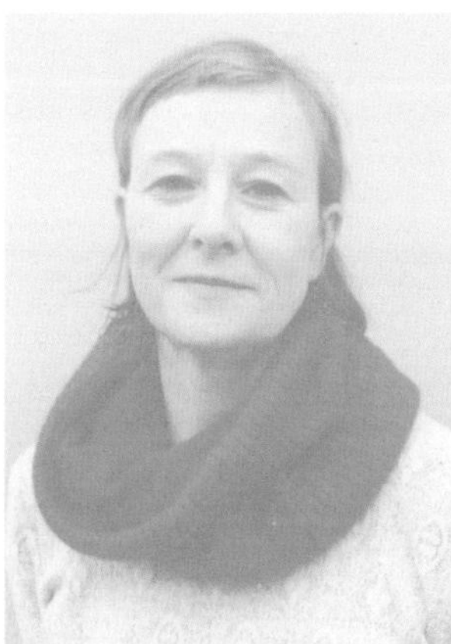

Petra Roggel

Petra Roggel ist diplomierte Wirtschaftswissenschaftlerin und Tänzerin. Sie arbeitete in den 1990er-Jahren am Theater am Halleschen Ufer in Berlin, bevor sie sich in der freien Szene Berlins selbstständig machte und mit Choreografen wie Xavier Le Roy, Thomas Lehmen oder Eszter Salamon zusammenarbeitete. Mehrere Jahre leitete sie zusammen mit Johan Reyniers das Kaaitheater in Brüssel und wechselte dann als Expertin für Tanz und Performance zur Zentrale des Goethe-Instituts in München, wo sie die Goethe-Institute weltweit beriet. Seit 2015 ist sie Leiterin des Goethe-Instituts Chicago.

Christina Wildgrube

Christina Wildgrube was born in 1983 in Wittenberg and works as a communication designer. She graduated in 2011 from the University of Applied Sciences Berlin. During her studies she spent one semester at the University of Illinois at Chicago to work on her book "820,154 footprints," a project on the analogies of the city of Chicago and its typography. In September 2018, she graduated from the Academy of Fine Arts Leipzig, writing her dissertation on "LAND SETZEN – 11 Druckgrafiken im Handsatz." In her work, she focuses on print techniques in landscapes. Siedlung Törten *will be shown in "kunstRaum22" at the Anhaltischer Kunstverein in Dessau in late 2019. Wildgrube lives and works in Leipzig.*

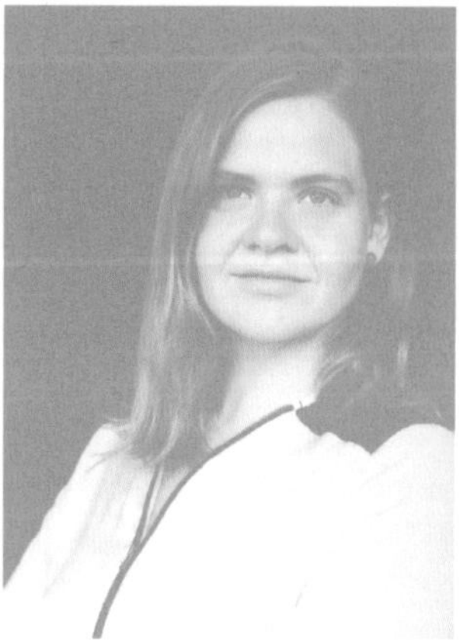

Christina Wildgrube

Christina Wildgrube wurde 1983 in Wittenberg geboren und arbeitet als Kommunikationsdesignerin. 2011 schloss sie ihr Studium an der University of Applied Sciences in Berlin ab. Während eines Auslandssemesters an der University of Illinois in Chicago arbeitete sie an ihrem Buch 820,154 footprints, *einem Projekt über die Analogien der Stadt Chicago und ihre Typografie. Im September 2018 schloss sie ihr Studium an der Hochschule für Grafik und Buchkunst mit der Arbeit* LAND SETZEN – 11 Druckgrafiken im Handsatz *ab. Den Schwerpunkt ihrer Arbeit legt sie auf Drucktechniken im Bereich von Landschaftsmotiven.* Siedlung Törten *wird Ende 2019 im „kunstRaum22“ des Anhaltischen Kunstvereins in Dessau gezeigt. Wildgrube lebt und arbeitet in Leipzig.*

Rebecca Wilton

Rebecca Wilton was born in 1979 and lives and works in Berlin, Germany. She studied Photography at the Academy of Fine Arts Leipzig under Timm Rautert. Aside from her art projects, which have been shown in numerous group and solo exhibitions, she has been involved in many different projects in recent years, such as working as editor at Camera Austria International and curating independent shows in public spaces, e.g. the 2015–16 series Sundowner at Neue Nationalgalerie in Berlin. She currently works as an artist, author, and editor in Berlin.

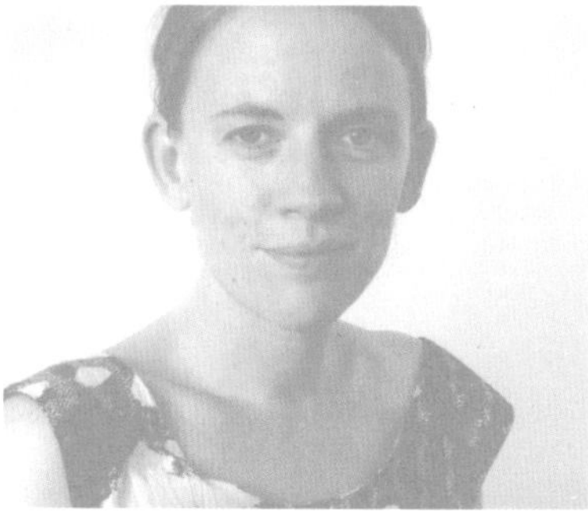

Rebecca Wilton

Rebecca Wilton, 1979 geboren, lebt und arbeitet in Berlin. Sie studierte unter Timm Rautert Fotografie an der Hochschule für Grafik und Buchkunst Leipzig. Neben ihren Kunstprojekten, die im Rahmen zahlreicher Gemeinschafts- und Einzelausstellungen gezeigt wurden, widmete sie sich in den vergangenen Jahren verschiedensten Aufgaben. Hierzu gehörten Tätigkeiten als Redakteurin für Camera Austria International *und als Kuratorin für unabhängige Ausstellungen im öffentlichen Raum, darunter 2015/16 die Reihe* Sundowner *an der Neuen Nationalgalerie in Berlin. Gegenwärtig ist sie als Künstlerin, Autorin und Redakteurin in Berlin tätig.*

1 **Serene Wise**

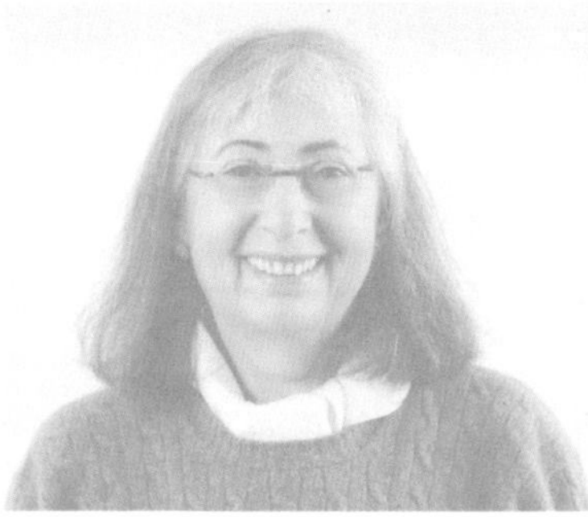

Serene Wise studied Art and Design at the School of the Art Institute of Chicago and the University of Michigan. She is a graduate of the University of Wisconsin, Madison (B.A.), the University of Chicago (M.A.), and the University of Michigan, Ann Arbor (M.U.P., A. Alfred Taubman College of Architecture and Urban Planning). In 2017 she was the City of Chicago International Sister Cities Program artist-in-residence in Lucerne, Switzerland, where she exhibited at Das Gelbe Haus. She was also artist-in-residence at the Cité Internationale des Arts, Paris, France, and the Chicago Artists' Coalition, Coalition Gallery, Chicago, and scholar-in-residence at the University of Chicago. Wise's solo exhibition venues include the American Library in Paris, France; Chelsea Gallery, Old Town Hall, London, United Kingdom; and in Chicago. She lives and works in Chicago.

Serene Wise

Serene Wise studierte Kunst und Design an der School of the Art Institute of Chicago und der University of Michigan. Sie ist Absolventin der University of Wisconsin, Madison (B.A.), der University of Chicago (M.A.) und der University of Michigan, Ann Arbor (M.U.P., A. Alfred Taubman College of Architecture and Urban Planning). 2017 war sie im Rahmen des City of Chicago International Sister Cities Program Artist-in-Residence im Schweizer Luzern, wo sie in Das Gelbe Haus ausstellte. Außerdem war sie Artist-in-Residence in der Cité internationale des Arts, Paris und der Chicago Artists' Coalition, Coalition Gallery, Chicago, und Scholar-in-Residence an der University of Chicago. Einzelausstellungen von Serene Wise wurden in der American Library in Paris, in der Chelsea Gallery, Old Town Hall, London und in Chicago gezeigt. Sie lebt und arbeitet in Chicago.

Monika Wulfers

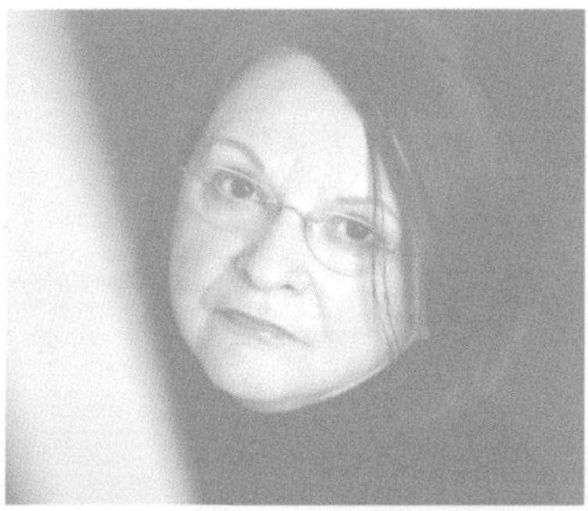

Born in Berlin, Monika Wulfers works and lives in Chicago. She earned a B.A. in Philosophy from North Central College, Naperville, and an M.F.A. from the School of the Art Institute of Chicago, where she studied Film under Stan Brakhage and Painting under Ray Yoshida and Ted Halkin. She has made significant contributions in art and technology and advanced the use of the computer as an artistic medium. Recent light sculptures, paintings, and drawings parallel mathematical systems she uses in her work with computers. Her work has been shown in museums in the US and internationally and is included in the permanent collections of the Elmhurst Art Museum, DePaul University, Wilhelm-Hack-Museum, Argonne National Laboratory, Museum of Contemporary Art, Chicago, as well as numerous private collections.

Monika Wulfers

Die in Berlin geborene Monika Wulfers lebt und arbeitet in Chicago. Sie erwarb am North Central College in Naperville (USA) einen B.A. in Philosophie und an der School of the Art Institute of Chicago einen M.F.A. Sie leistete bedeutende Beiträge im Bereich Kunst und Technologie und förderte den Einsatz des Computers als Medium der Kunst. Ihren neueren Lichtskulpturen, Gemälden und Zeichnungen liegen parallele mathematische Systeme aus ihrer Arbeit mit dem Computer zugrunde. Ihre Arbeiten wurden in US-amerikanischen und internationalen Museen gezeigt und gehören zur ständigen Sammlung des Elmhurst Art Museum, der DePaul University, des Wilhelm-Hack-Museums, des Argonne National Laboratory, des Museum of Contemporary Art in Chicago sowie zu zahlreichen Privatsammlungen.

Ingrid Zeller

Ingrid Zeller is Professor of Instruction in the German Department at Northwestern University. Originally from Munich, she studied Piano Performance at Manhattan School of Music (B.M.) and pursued graduate work in German Studies at Columbia University (M.A.) in New York City. In 2009, she was certified as a volunteer docent for the Chicago Architecture Center. She gives walking tours with a focus on the Bauhaus and has been involved in numerous online and onsite projects related to the Bauhaus. She teaches a course on Bauhaus and Beyond: German Influences on the Chicago Skyline *at Northwestern and holds frequent presentations and workshops on the topic. Currently the president of the Northern Illinois AATG (American Association for Teachers of German), she has received numerous awards for her engagement, including the Goethe-Institut/AATG Certificate of Merit.*

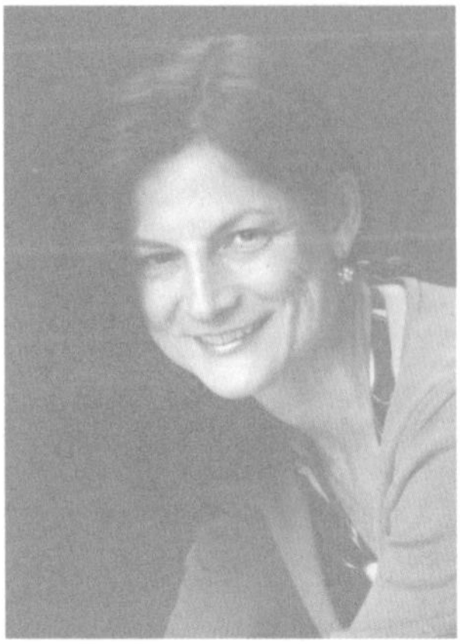

Ingrid Zeller

Ingrid Zeller ist außerordentliche Professorin am Deutschen Institut der Northwestern University. Ursprünglich aus München stammend, studierte sie an der Manhattan School of Music Pianistik (B.M.) und absolvierte dann ein Germanistikstudium an der Columbia University (M.A.) in New York. 2009 erhielt sie die Zulassung als ehrenamtliche Mitarbeiterin beim Chicago Architecture Center. Sie konzipiert Führungen zum Thema Bauhaus und ist an einer Vielzahl von Online- und Onsite-Projekten in diesem Bereich beteiligt. An der Northwestern University leitet sie den Kurs „Bauhaus and Beyond: German Influences on the Chicago Skyline" und bietet hierzu auch Präsentationen und Workshops an. Als amtierende Vorsitzende der AATG (American Association for Teachers of German) für den Bereich Nord-Illinois erhielt sie zahlreiche Auszeichnungen für ihr Engagement, unter anderem das vom Goethe-Institut/AATG verliehene „Certificate of Merit".

Colophon / Impressum

This publication was published as part of the exhibition
A Little Piece of Bauhaus *at the Goethe-Institut Chicago*
05/02/2016–12/31/2018
Diese Publikation erscheint anlässlich der Ausstellung
A Little Piece of Bauhaus *am Goethe-Institut Chicago*
02/05/2016–31/12/2018

Editor / Herausgeber
Petra Roggel, Goethe-Institut Chicago

Editorial staff / Redaktion
Petra Roggel, Irmi Maunu-Kocian, Nicole Schmid

Copyediting / Lektorat
Ilka Backmeister-Collacott (DE), Jeremy Gaines (EN)

Translations / Übersetzungen
Angela Selter, Faith Ann Gibson

Design / Gestaltung
Harri Kuhn, mischen, Berlin

Photo credit / Fotonachweis

Page 1 clockwise / Seite 1 im Uhrzeigersinn
Christina Wildgrube, Assaf Evron, Rebecca Wilton, Doug Fogelson, Heike Albrecht

Page 144 clockwise / Seite 144 im Uhrzeigersinn
Serene Wise, Assaf Evron, Luftwerk, Anke Loh, Monika Wulfers

11/12 *INsite, Luftwerk 2014, photo: Kate Joyce;* ***25/26*** *Mies Windows – Crown Hall, Chicago, 2017, Assaf Evron, photo: Assaf Evron;* ***33/34*** *La Fayette, 2014, Rebecca Wilton, photo: Rebecca Wilton;* ***43/44*** *Siedlung Törten, 2017, Christina Wildgrube, photo: Christina Wildgrube;* ***55/56*** *Interknit, 2018, Anke Loh, photo: James Prinz Photography;* ***65/66*** *Forms & Records, 2014–2015, Doug Fogelson, photo: Doug Fogelson;* ***75/76*** *Collages, 2017–2018, Assaf Evron, photo: Assaf Evron;* ***85/86*** *Studies in Grays and White, #6, 2013, Serene Wise, photo: Denise Elsman;* ***94/95*** *Summer I (Detail), 2005, Serene Wise, photo: Denise Elsman;* ***96*** *Summer I, 2005, Serene Wise, photo: Adam Biba;* ***97*** *Summer II, 2005, Serene Wise, photo: Adam Biba;* ***99/100*** *Trace Movement / Bewegungsspuren, 2018, Heike Albrecht, photo: Heike Albrecht;* ***111/112*** *Lines and Numbers, Random 1881, 2018, Monika Wulfers, photo: Monika Wulfers;* ***119/120*** *Screenshot of a Skype conversation between Petra Roggel (Chicago) and Harri Kuhn (Berlin) about concept and design of this publication / Screenshot eines Skypegesprächs zwischen Petra Roggel (Chicago) und Harri Kuhn (Berlin) über Konzept und Entwurf dieser Publikation, 2018, photo: Harri Kuhn*

Biografien / Biographies
Heike Albrecht, photo: Heike Albrecht; Franz Anton Cramer, photo: Sarah Edgehill; Assaf Evron, photo: Assaf Evron; Doug Fogelson, photo: Chester Alamo Costello; Anke Loh, photo: James Prinz Photography; Kristina Lowis, photo: Julien Trillat; Luftwerk, photo: Kate Joyce; Petra Roggel, photo: Denise Elsman; Christina Wildgrube, photo: Julia Stiller; Rebecca Wilton, photo: Rebecca Wilton; Serene Wise, photo: Assaf Evron; Monika Wulfers, photo: Mieke Zuiderweg; Ingrid Zeller, photo: Ingrid Zeller

Project management / Projektmanagement, Kerber Verlag
Claudia Voigtländer

Production / Herstellung, Kerber Verlag
Jens Bartneck

The Deutsche Nationalbibliothek lists this publication in the Deutsche Nationalbibliografie; detailed bibliographic data are available on the Internet at http://dnb.dnb.de.
Die Deutsche Nationalbibliothek verzeichnet diese Publikation in der Deutschen Nationalbibliografie; detaillierte bibliografische Daten sind im Internet über http://dnb.dnb.de abrufbar.

Printed and published by / Gesamtherstellung und Vertrieb

Kerber Verlag, Bielefeld
Windelsbleicher Str. 166–170
33659 Bielefeld
Germany
Tel. +49 (0) 5 21/9 50 08-10
Fax +49 (0) 5 21/9 50 08-88
info@kerberverlag.com

Kerber, US Distribution
ARTBOOK | D.A.P.
75 Broad Street, Suite 630
New York, NY 10004
Tel. +1 (212) 627-1999
Fax +1 (212) 627-9484

Kerber publications are available in selected bookstores and museum shops worldwide (distributed in Europe, Asia, South and North America).
Kerber-Publikationen werden weltweit in führenden Buchhandlungen und Museumsshops angeboten (Vertrieb in Europa, Asien, Nord- und Südamerika).

All rights reserved. No part of this publication may be reproduced, translated, stored in a retrieval system or transmitted in any form or by any means, electronic, mechanical, photocopying or recording or otherwise, without the prior permission of the publisher.
Alle Rechte, insbesondere das Recht auf Vervielfältigung und Verbreitung sowie Übersetzung, vorbehalten. Kein Teil dieses Werkes darf in irgendeiner Form ohne schriftliche Genehmigung des Verlages reproduziert werden oder unter Verwendung elektronischer Systeme verarbeitet, vervielfältigt oder verbreitet werden.

© 2019 Kerber Verlag, Bielefeld/Berlin, artist and authors / Künstler und Autoren, for the works by / für die Werke von Rebecca Wilton: Artists Rights Society (ARS), New York, 2019

ISBN 978-3-7356-0606-8
www.kerberverlag.com

Printed in Germany

This publication was made possible with the support of
Diese Publikation wurde unterstützt von

FRIENDS OF GOETHE CHICAGO

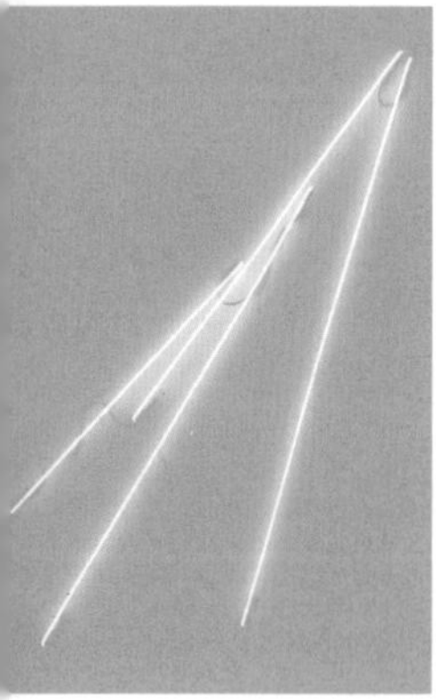

EIN STÜCK BAUHAUS

Ein Ausstellungsprojekt des Goethe-Instituts Chicago, mit Arbeiten von Heike Albrecht, Franz Anton Cramer, Assaf Evron, Doug Fogelson, Anke Loh, Kristina Lowis, Luftwerk, Christina Wildgrube, Rebecca Wilton, Serene Wise, Monika Wulfers und Ingrid Zeller

An exhibition project at the Goethe-Institut Chicago with works by Heike Albrecht, Franz Anton Cramer, Assaf Evron, Doug Fogelson, Anke Loh, Kristina Lowis, Luftwerk, Christina Wildgrube, Rebecca Wilton, Serene Wise, Monika Wulfers, and Ingrid Zeller

24,00 € (D)

9 783735 606068

www.kerberverlag.com

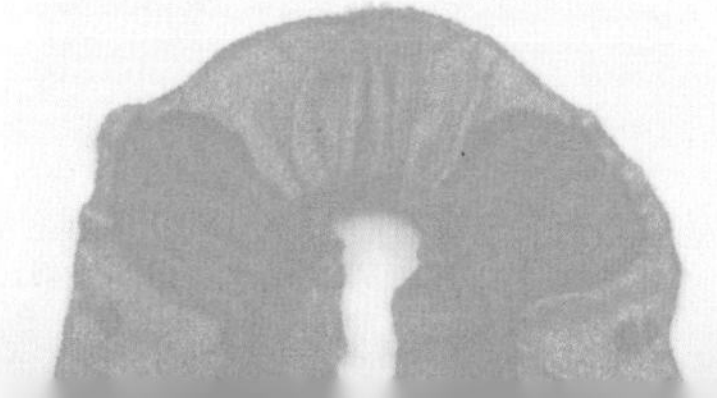

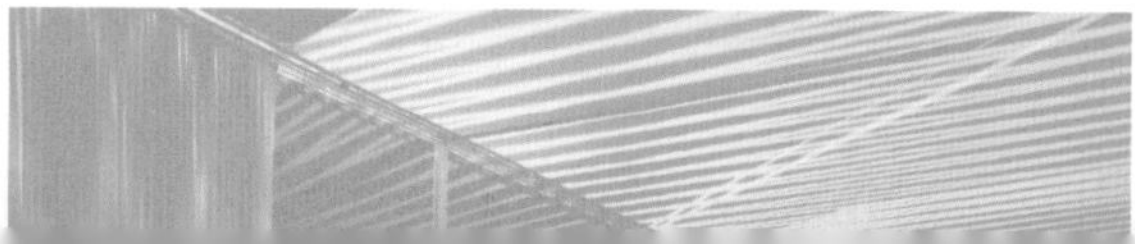